TO THE LOVES OF MY LIFE

Eileen — My Bride, my helpmate, my best friend, the mother of my children, and the one who proved she would love me unconditionally and forever. I am so glad that we are "just passing through together." You taught me to trust, to love, and the hardest thing ... to be loved. You have seen the best and worst of me, and you still love me.

My five children:
- The Honorable and Virtuous one
- The Peaceful one, God's Gift
- The Joyful Flowering one covered in Beauty
- The Devoted one to God, who is a Woman of God
- The one who has the Strength of God

You each have loved me and in doing so you have taught me to love.

ENDORSEMENT

"After a career as a soldier in the US Army's Special Operations Forces, I've learned to be very careful about who I trust to my left and right. In SOF, you are measured by what you do, not what you say you can or will do. Victor is a man of his word and a man of action. I am proud to call him a partner and friend.

His story is an inspiration for all. The unbearable and systematic abuse that Victor survived has placed him in a unique position to reach others. His ministry is necessary, more than ever, reaching the lost and confronting the manifestation of evil in our time. He's confronted evil across the world and does it with understanding, compassion, and grace but also with confidence and the expectation that justice prevails.

I've worked with Victor and his team in the Middle East and they are succeeding where others fear to tread. The widows, orphans, exploited, and oppressed are still in need and calling for our help. The command God sent out to His followers to heed this call is as true today as it was thousands of years ago. But so few answer this call. Victor, Eileen, the Marx family, and his team are on the frontlines, in the trenches, figuratively and literally, rescuing the oppressed and providing hope to so many.

Guardian Group is proud to be a strategic partner with Victor Marx Ministries.

Read his story, let your self be moved to action and join us in the fight to bring freedom to the oppressed."

Jeff Tiegs
LTC (Ret.)
Special Forces
Guardian Group COO

ACKNOWLEDGEMENTS

To my mother who gave me the gift of life, taught me the value of humor, and gave me an iron will to never give up. You are loved more than you will ever know this side of heaven! You are a princess warrior, a true and rare intercessor. You have risen above what you endured as a child to be victorious in Christ.

To my dad. You had the courage to come back into your kid's life, restoring "the years that the locusts had stolen." Your godly courage is what the Lord used to bring me to Him. You taught me the value of following Christ with all my heart, soul, and strength. You are a Godly Warrior. You helped me become a man!

To my siblings Tony, Mike, Debbie, Twyla, and Chermayne. You each endured, survived, and rose above what we all went through. My story is simply one ray of light shining through the prism of our childhood. I have wept much while thinking of what you endured in your own journey, and you will never know how proud I am of you. I pray that you know the God of all mercy and the Prince of Peace's love, comfort, and healing touch. You can trust HIM. I would not have wanted anyone else on our childhood team besides y'all. We did it!!

To Wayne Atcheson who bird-dogged me with gentleness and persistence to put my story in book form to help more people. Wayne, you truly are one of the most godly and disciplined men I have ever known. Thank you.

To Alan Maki and Tom Calabrese for your revisions, and to James Werning for the final edits and additions. To my contributing editors, David and Karen Turner, Elaine Humphries, Diane Mitchell, and Trudy Thomas (editor of the 2nd and 3rd revised and expanded editions.)

What gifts you each have been in this journey. May the Lord Himself bless you beyond your wildest expectations!

To Dr. Arlys McDonald for her gifted counseling at the McDonald Therapy center in Vista, California. Your concern for those who have been abused and abandoned reflects the compassionate Father Heart of God. To Dominic Herbst, so much wisdom into hurting hearts needing hope.

To each man I have named as my pastor: Brian Broderson, Mark Galvin, Bill Stonebreaker, Steve Holt, Al Pittman, Albert Fuentes, Mike Clark, and Brian Bell. Thank you for your friendship and investment in my life.

To the Men in Ministry who have touched my life in significant ways: Chuck Smith, Danny Lehman, Greg Laurie, Raul Ries, Mike MacIntosh, Ray Bentley, David Rosales, Jeff Gill, Ron Hindt, Gaylord Tohill and Mike Rueffert who brought me into my first youth prison and introduced me to the great need of our day. To Fabian Loo: We share the same birthdate, anniversary, and most important same and only Savior, Jesus!

It's a rare gift to find true friends in this life. I am very fortunate and grateful to those whom I count as such. You know who you are!!

Special thanks to the "Honor Guard" of ATP who make this ministry possible through your prayers and financial support. You are awesome warriors to stand shoulder-to-shoulder within this battle against darkness at the gates of hell.

To every believer who has ever shown me Jesus Christ with skin on. You have increased my faith.

To every child, teen, and adult who has endured the stuff of life that is not supposed to happen. I commend each of you for not giving up and having the tremendous courage to move from surviving to living. It can be a painful, scary journey, but it is worth every step. Remember that you can trust Jesus. He will never leave you or forsake you. (Hebrews 13:5) He loves you!

Finally, to every prayer warrior and ministry partner and staff member who has made All Things Possible Ministries a reality and a spiritual war machine for the kingdom of God! Just wait until you see all your treasures in heaven and they each have a name.

FORWARD

by Karl William Marx Sr., Tenth Degree Black Belt and Keichu-Do Karate Grandmaster

This is the story of Victor – he was the son of a pimping, drug dealing, street fighter, involved in the Cajun Mafia. Victor wanted nothing to do with his dad – that's me – and you can't blame him. I wanted nothing to do with him either.

What hope is there in life for a kid raised in those kinds of circumstances? Not much, that's for sure. But that don't mean he can't have a happy ending in life, because our God is a God who brings hope to the hopeless.

Victor was as hopeless as can be – the son of a hopeless father. He's got quite a story to tell – a story of abuse and abandonment and rage and lawlessness, but all that junk is gone today. How did it happen? Well, Victor is going to tell you all about it. Hold onto your hat, though, because his story will take you on a wild ride from hell to heaven and all points in between.

The main thing I want to say is that you might have your own issues of rage or defeat or hopelessness or abuse. You might be like Victor was – not giving a rip about your old man, seething with anger, maybe even ready to take somebody's head off. No matter. Somebody loves you just the same. Somebody is waiting patiently for you to find peace for your anxious soul. Miracles do happen and they can happen to you. How do I know? Because that's exactly what happened to both Victor and me, and I don't know of any guys meaner or worse off than we were.

So I consider this an honor and a privilege to introduce my son Victor to you. He's a good man – I'm proud of him and I love him like a father should, even if we both had a rough start in life. God's forgiveness and love is powerful enough to cover a world of sin and shame. That's what He's done for Victor and me, and He wants to do the same for you. Hear my son out. Give him your full attention. But make yourself good and comfortable first, because you won't want to stop reading once you get started.

Karl William Marx Sr.
American by birth
Cajun by nature
Christian by choice
Warrior for Jesus Christ

A TRIBUTE FROM A SON TO HIS DAD

Murrieta, California, February 14, 2013: It's a funny thing sitting here, actually fully immersed in the moment that I have rehearsed in my head many, many times. The moment I find out my dad has gone Home. I got the call at exactly 1:41 am on February 14th, 2013. I was not asleep but actually wide awake, visiting with my wife after a wonderful evening dinner and an earlier call from my dad's sweet wife of 15 years who called me from his phone at 6:38 pm on the evening of the 13th. She was alarmed and concerned as he had a pretty rough afternoon between 3:00 and 6:00. Apparently, he had blacked out but seemed okay outside of some odd behavior. She told me he then, for the first time in their 15 years of marriage, said he was going to bed around 6:30 pm. He was struggling with a bout of old anxiety, his lifetime foe and surely his thorn in the flesh. He said he always looked at this challenge as a person and real enemy and instead of being defeated he used it to make him a prayer warrior and that, I can say, he surely was. Kathy helped his pain-riddled body to bed, tucked him in nice and comfy, and put on the only radio station he listed to: Christian Bible teaching and worship. He was able to settle in and drift to sleep after wrestling with his CPAP machine. Then our Heavenly Father granted my dad his request to come take him home in his sleep. His wife would find him already gone. She tried to resuscitate him, but God's will had already been done.

I have always wondered how I would react or respond to my Dad's death. I can write that I feel a sense of gratitude toward the Lord and that His name is worthy to be praised; that Heaven is more real to me now than it was a few hours ago; that the truth is like I heard Greg Laurie say live yesterday on the radio with Pastor Chuck, that our days are numbered which I really, really got it in a new way. That we do not have to fear or worry about death but only live fully knowing when our service to the Lord is complete on this earth, that He will bring us, usher us, grant us the most magnificent Homecoming and grand entrance. A Homecoming that instantly relieves us of all pain, suffering, torment, worry, insecurity, fear, replaced with a permanent peace, comfort, and love that have all been fulfilled by our living Hope Jesus and His death on the Cross and resurrection.

I lay here typing thinking what is he seeing right now; my dad's new eyes are able to fully and completely look upon the Throne of God and embrace his Savior, the One who delivered him from a life of sin, and now has transformed his corruption into incorruption. My eyes fill with tears trying to type, my jaws tightening a bit knowing full well my dad has fallen on his knees and is overwhelmed by the Lord's Love, amazing Love. Looking up he is being greeted and jumped on by the hundreds of those whom he had boldly proclaimed his faith to in person and I'm sure the thousands indirectly through prayers and our film that have gone before him.

"Oh death," I say, "Where is your sting? Your brief appearance at my father's bed was the last perception of sin he would be bothered with but for a moment; and you, Satan, did not win by the death of a saint, a warrior. No! You lost because his race has been run, his battles all fought, and he got the last word - YES LORD!! as he heard Jesus say, 'Welcome Home, good and faithful servant, enter into your rest!'"

Thank you, dad, for bringing me to know the love of our Heavenly Father by rejecting passivity, accepting responsibility, warring for me to come to salvation on June 22, 1986. Thank you for allowing me to change my last name back to yours and carry on our family name and legacy; for being my best man in my wedding; for teaching me and training me in Keichu-Do which you created; for helping me become a man; for always being there for me with an instant prayer and those amazing healing prayers of peace that NEVER once failed to comfort me in my greatest times of struggle; for your laughter and love for the Lord.

TABLE OF CONTENTS

A POEM

You Are Who You Are for a Reason
by Russell Kelfer

You are who you are for a reason.
You're part of an intricate plan.
You're a precious and perfect unique design,
Called God's special woman or man.

You look like you look for a reason.
Our God made no mistake.
He knit you together within the womb,
You're just what he wanted to make.

The parents you had were the ones he chose,
And no matter how you may feel,
They were custom-designed with God's plan in mind,
And they bear the Master's seal.

No, that trauma you faced was not easy.
And God wept that it hurt you so;
But it was allowed to shape your heart
So that into his likeness you'd grow.

You are who you are for a reason,
You've been formed by the Master's rod.
You are who you are, beloved,
Because there is a God!

chapter one

HE AIN'T MY KID

Those were Daddy's first words when he found out that my mom was pregnant with me. No hugs and kisses for Momma. No cigars for the neighbors. No words of praise for the future All Star Champion and President of the United States. (That's me, in case you're wondering.) No, he only welcomed me with denial.

"He ain't my kid."

If there had been a window on the womb, here's what I would have seen the last night my parents were together. I would have watched my dad in a rage, pinning my mother to a bed and trying to shove rosary beads down her throat. He ended up punching a hole through the wall instead of my mother. Not exactly what you'd call the happy couple. You see, Billy and Rita Marx's love was stone cold dead at the same time that my little life was just starting to develop.

My parents had the classic "three D" marital symptoms that included drama, disaster, and divorce. That's pretty much what you'd expect when an abused sixteen-year-old swamp girl from southern Louisiana gets tangled up with a man who has received so much anger and violence that he cannot possibly contain it.

Hey. This is Victor and I'm going to share some thoughts here from time to time. God intended couples to marry for a lifetime. Marriage is not meant to be a temporary arrangement. What's more, the Bible talks about the importance of saving sexual intimacy until marriage. How about you? If you're dating, how can you actually focus on the qualities of the other person's heart, like honesty, integrity, and faithfulness, rather than on the qualities that are only skin-deep? Is your relationship pure and pleasing to God? If you are married, how can you see the good in your spouse and not get wrapped up in petty surface issues? Or if you have serious problems in your marriage, how can you get the help you need from a pastor or a counselor before it's too late?

Since birth, they had both been buried under mountains of violence, abuse, abandonment, neglect, rejection, and hopelessness. Nothing short of God's miraculous healing power could have enabled them to live any differently.

My mother Rita never really loved my dad, nor did she have the capacity to do so. How could she, when she had never been shown what true love really is? Her French and Spanish parents gave her those beautiful dark eyes, hair and skin, but who could she trust to love and cherish her? This sweet girl was robbed of her innocence at an early age by a wicked abductor. As a teenager, she was raped by an adult "friend of the family." This is how she learned to see men – as the abusers. This is also why she found it impossible to truly love any man.

Then when you look at my father, you really see the Lord's hand of protection on my mother and us kids. Billy Marx grew up without a strong male role model to teach him how to deal with the difficulties of life, without a man who could show him how to accept responsibility. He didn't have a clue how to treat women with respect and honor and love. His troubled upbringing only got worse when he was placed in a boys' home. No wonder things went from bad to worse with his teenage bride.

It is safe to say that my father had some significant emotional issues. He often took great pleasure in inflicting pain and suffering on others. He was a feared street fighter whose nickname was "Le Tigre" or "The Tiger." He fought hard, drank hard, and broke laws hard. Eventually, he became involved with the Cajun Mafia. He was a pimp's pimp. He would take advantage of girls who were struggling and teach them how to "play the game" to make money. Then after their "training" was over, he would sell them to other pimps.

He also scammed insurance companies with fake accidents. This racket eventually grew so big that it included fake victims, crooked doctors, lying lawyers, and more. Naturally, he dealt in drugs. He was also a cooler, which is a head bouncer who trains other bouncers. This guy had power and he commanded a lot of fear and respect. After I was born, his organization and nearly everyone he worked with were busted. When I was a child I almost never saw the man. Later he was deeply involved in the occult, becoming a Warlock who dealt in some bad scary stuff. But with all his faults he actually loved his children in the best way he knew how... from a distance.

After my parents divorced, my mother continued her bad habit of choosing the wrong men. The next guy was a known thug who ran a club and was involved in the dark side of crime. You'd think my father wouldn't care – he hated my mother and he didn't want anything to do with me. But what did he decide to do? He simply did what every self-respecting criminal would do. He set out to kill the competition.

First my father called my grandmother to vent his rage and possibly to say his final goodbye. She calmed him down and then suggested that they meet next to the sheriff's office, of all places. For some strange reason my father agreed, and when they met the law stepped in and arrested him. My father wasn't the sharpest tool in the shed. (Maybe I got my brains from him.)

I always felt sad knowing that my father didn't want me. Maybe you know the feeling. The great thing is that in God's eyes, no child is unwanted. He loves us all with an incredible love!

"Your eyes saw me when I was only a fetus. Every day of my life was recorded in Your book before one of them had taken place."
– Psalm 139:16 (Unless otherwise noted, all Bible quotations are from God's Word ®. See title page for more information.)
"I know the plans that I have for you, declares the Lord. They are plans for peace and not disaster, plans to give you a future filled with hope." – Jeremiah 29:11

I think my grandmother convinced the police that my father was mentally deranged, because they ended up putting him in the Pineville, Louisiana state mental institution for observation. His own father had died in this same institution. I'm sure that fact motivated him to get out of there as quickly as possible. Eight weeks later he was released back into his life of crime. He began to challenge other thugs for control. Soon the situation grew more dangerous for everyone. The fuse was lit. It was just a matter of time before the powder keg exploded.

My father still could not let go of his sinister plan to murder my mother's boyfriend, so he put a pistol in his pocket and drove to that guy's favorite bar. Fortunately for the man and for my father, he wasn't there. My father never missed an opportunity to fuel his rage with alcohol, so he waited and drank. The waitress spiked one of my father's drinks because the next thing he remembered was waking up in the parking lot of the Purple Peacock Bar across town. I guess it wasn't my father's time to die. I remembered this incident later in life when I too had several close calls with death. I always asked myself that same question. "Why wasn't this my time to die?"

A week later my father was talking to a couple of deputies and they dared him to shoot and kill my mother's boyfriend. They said they'd call it self-defense. Daddy figured it was a double cross and soon he lost all interest in killing the guy. He also lost interest in my mom and his family. He went his way and we went ours. Years would pass before I would meet him.

chapter two

A Birth, Two Deaths, and a Marriage

Given the chaotic circumstances surrounding my conception, my mother could have easily justified an abortion – had that option been available to her. I thank the Lord she did not. I was born July 5, 1965, with a birth deformity called funnel chest or pectus excavatum. Basically, my chest was concave. I was a small sickly boy and Momma stayed with me in the Lourdes Hospital in Lafayette, Louisiana, for two weeks. Then we went to Grandma Cook's nursing home where two brothers and a sister awaited my arrival. Tony was five, Mike was four, and Debbie was two.

In spite of her difficult circumstances, my mother loved being a mom and cared a lot for us kids. She was only twenty-two and she was forced to get right back to work as a beautician while we stayed in the back of a nursing home or with friends. While Momma worked fourteen-hour days, my siblings and I found ourselves with a young African-American girl who took wonderful care of us. Today I'm so thankful for her and for the nanny, because they inadvertently prevented us from being infected by the extreme prejudice between blacks and whites that existed then and sadly still exists now in many areas of the South.

When I was eighteen months old Momma lost her two brothers. At age eighteen, Lionel contracted rheumatic fever and died of pneumonia and heart failure after a few days in the hospital. Then about a month later, Victor Jay, age twenty-four, lost control of his street-racing mustang on a bridge and landed upside down in a creek. His head got pinned under six inches of water and he drowned. These two deaths devastated Momma. She loved her brothers deeply – she had even named me after Victor Jay.

In later years I could sense a melancholy look in my relatives' eyes when they called me "Victor Jay." He was a good man.

Through my Momma's struggle with these untimely deaths, she developed a longing in her heart to know God. She began searching for a relationship with Jesus Christ. She was also feeling overwhelmed with four children to support and she actually had to let her Aunt Dora take care of us for a while. Momma cried many nights because it hurt her so much to give us up. But she knew that one day she would get us all back together again.

After many months, Momma met a man who was to become her second husband. Mr. K. was a former military man. He had been trained by the National Security Agency – at least that's what he told us. In a conflict, his task was to go on covert operations. He would get dropped behind enemy lines with instructions to extract information and eliminate key enemies. Mr. K. claimed that he was sent into missions armed with only a boot knife and a wire with grips on both ends, to kill his enemies by stabbing, strangling, or even decapitation. What a job! I don't know if he was lying, but I sure believed it was true.

When I was three years old, Mr. K. married my mother. I suppose we had high hopes because finally our family was reunited and provided for in our hour of need. After the wedding, our family settled in Lafayette, hoping to "live happily ever after." My stepfather began working in sales and all seemed good. Little did we know that our new father – who had a college degree, loved Ernest Hemingway novels, and had a great mastery of the English language – would dump some serious problems on us that would nearly destroy our family.

God planned for families to be led by two people – a mom and a dad – but unfortunately it doesn't always work out that way. It's tough surviving in a broken home, and kids often feel abandoned or rejected by a dad or a mom. Maybe you know what it's like. If so, I hope the following Bible verses will encourage you. God will always come through in the end!

"Even if my father and mother abandon me, the Lord will take care of me." – Psalm 27:10

"Be strong and courageous. Don't tremble! Don't be afraid of them! The Lord your God is the one who is going with you. He won't abandon you or leave you." – Deuteronomy 31:6

---

chapter three

THE DEVIL IN THE DRINK

Mr. K. had begun his marriage to my mother on the right foot. He even quoted John 3:16 from the Bible to her: *For God so loved the world that He gave his one and only Son, that whoever believes in Him shall not perish but have eternal life.* Momma liked that because faith in God meant a lot to her, especially in the hard times. She remembered the Sunday she had gone to Northside Baptist Church in Lafayette and made a commitment to Jesus Christ. But Momma's hopes for a church-going family were derailed when her new husband's dark side was revealed.

Mr. K. was an alcoholic and his drinking scared all of us to death. Some people get silly and stupid when they drink. Not this man. He would get mean and violent. He was regularly unfaithful to my mother. There's much worse stuff that he'd do, but I'll tell you about that later.

When we lived in Hattiesburg, Mississippi, my Momma decided she had had enough. She suspected that he was cheating with one of her best friends, and sure enough she caught them red handed in a motel room. Out of respect for my Momma, I will not tell you all the details of that event. Let me just say that my stepfather always seemed to get away with his evil, but the cheating woman did not get off so easy. I think you get the picture.

I'm not sure why, but my Momma stuck with this man for several years despite the cheating. They even had two daughters. I loved my little sisters, even though I was mean to them at times. I guess when you "see mean" all the time in your father, you're more likely to follow the example and act mean yourself, which is what I did. Mr. K. eventually left sales and became a bail bondsman. The word around town was that when guys didn't pay him back, he'd beat them up until they gave him what they owed. This was how our new dad supported his family of eight. Great way to bring home the bacon, isn't it?

Why do you think it's so hard not to follow the bad example of your parents? Maybe, because it's impossible for any human being to be good ... at least without the help of God. That's what the Bible says.

"The human mind is the most deceitful of all things. It is incurable. No one can understand how deceitful it is." – Jeremiah 17:9

"We've all become unclean, and all our righteous acts are like permanently stained rags. All of us shrivel like leaves, and our sins carry us away like the wind." – Isaiah 64:6

"What a miserable person I am. Who will rescue me from my dying body? I thank God that our Lord Jesus Christ rescues me!" – Romans 7:24-25

Don't read this section if you're easily disturbed – just skip to the next chapter, okay? But some people who have been traumatized will find help by working through this difficult part of my story with me. I told you that Mr. K. claimed he had been trained in covert operations and methods of interrogation techniques. Well, he practiced torture and mind control on me when I was about 3 ½ & 7 years old. He also molested me. I wasn't his only victim, and I don't exactly know what he did to other kids. But with me his methods included suffocation, near drowning in the bathtub, sleep deprivation, and extreme physical pain administered so carefully that it left no marks or evidence. This was no petty stuff –just ask the trauma counselor I went to many years later. This little kid was face to face with some of the worst stuff that Satan has to offer.

Life is crazy when the person a child looks to as protector becomes the abuser. Suddenly nothing is safe or sane anymore. Like many abused and molested children, I developed ways of coping with this terror. I would sleep in secret places, under blankets in the cracks of couches or arm chairs so that he couldn't find me. My mind learned to dissociate itself from reality. It's called "splitting." My brain would split into different realities. In one compartment of my mind I was just a "regular" boy, carefree and fun loving. Then there was that other dark compartment – the awful reality of this abuse and torture. Somehow, I learned to shut it out and deny that dark reality. It's a coping skill that I used all the way into my adult years. As an adult, I eventually had to undergo the care of a psychiatrist and psychologists. But it eventually came back to haunt me through nightmares and flashbacks, anxiety, and panic-attacks. It's kind of like trying to hold a beach ball under water: you can do it for so long until a wave comes which causes the ball to pop up and out. If you think my life was off to a bad start, you're right. But that doesn't mean it couldn't get any worse.

"I can do everything through Christ Who strengthens me." – Philippians 4:13

Jesus rescues us from the curse of sin! Don't ever believe that you are trapped in the sins of your family. Jesus can rescue you and give you an amazing future!

You might be saying, "Victor – this is extremely disturbing. Why are you telling this part of your story?" Well, let me assure you that it's not an easy story to tell. For years I denied that it even happened to me. But the answer to your question is simple. I have met so many other people who have endured similar abuse. If I can offer any hope or encouragement to others, it is this: our God is merciful and loving. He is ready and eager to heal you and restore you. He can tenderly pick up the broken pieces of your life, bit by bit, and reshape them into beauty and strength. This is God's desire for you, my friend!

Don't be discouraged if your restoration looks hopeless. It took me a while to come to this place of healing. But I can say without a doubt, God is in the business of bringing joy and comfort and beauty! Isn't that awesome! Don't think for one moment that God brings bad things to people. That comes from Satan, the "prince of this world." (John 16:11) God is the One who miraculously turns everything bad into good in the end if we let Him.

"We know that all things work together for the good of those who love God – those whom He has called according to His plan." – Romans 8:28

"Even though you planned evil against me, God planned good to

come out of it. This was to keep many people alive, as He is doing now." – Genesis 50:20

To learn more about how God can heal you and restore beauty to your life, I encourage you to read Dr. McDonald's appendix at the back of this book. She has a lot of hope to offer hurting people.

Jesus wants to do the same for you! Listen to our Lord's beautiful words of encouragement for me and for you:

"The Spirit of the Sovereign Lord is upon me, because He has anointed me to preach good tidings to the poor; He has sent me to bind up the brokenhearted, to proclaim liberty to the captives, and release from darkness for the prisoners; to proclaim the year of the Lord's favor and the day of vengeance of our God; to comfort all who mourn; to provide for those who grieve in Zion, to bestow on them a crown of beauty instead of ashes, the oil of gladness instead of mourning, and a garment of praise instead of a spirit of despair. They will be called oaks of righteousness, a planting of the Lord for the display of His splendor." – Isaiah 61:1-3 (NIV)

chapter four

An Arctic Assault in Mississippi

When I was five years old, a terrible incident occurred from which I barely survived. We were living in Mississippi and I was spending the summer on a commercial chicken farm that belonged to the parents of my stepfather. One day I was playing outside barefoot, wearing overalls cut into shorts. For fun I stuck chicken feathers in a corncob and tossed it high up in the air, watching it whirly-bird down like a helicopter. A tenant worker came up to me and asked what I was doing. I told him I was just playing. "Let me show you something in this house," he said, pointing to a green concrete building that contained a big commercial cooler for storing eggs.

I had seen this man before. He lived with his parents down the road from my grandparents. They were dirt poor and they made what money they could collecting Coke bottles for their redemption value. The woman was over 300 pounds and her husband was a thin man who always smoked hand-rolled cigarettes. Their adult son was the man who lured me into this building. I always assumed he was a child of inbreeding because of his slight mental retardation. I didn't like how he smelled like chicken manure.

The green building was off-limits to me, but I went with this man out of childlike curiosity. Once inside the building – slam! – he shut the door behind us. Immediately I sensed that something was not right.

He said, "Let me tell you something. This is what we're gonna do and if you don't do it I'm gonna kill you."

Then he began to molest me.

I cried, "No, no, no!" I fought with my fists and kicked and screamed.

This man persisted, and he would not let me go. All the while I kept trying to fight him, but I was just a five-year-old kid. Finally, he dragged me to a large commercial cooler. He opened the door, threw me inside, and locked the big metal door.

I began pounding on the door, crying, and screaming for someone to rescue me. But the longer I pounded the more hopeless I became. Eventually I came to the harsh realization that no one was going to come to my rescue.

I'm going to freeze to death. It was a horrible revelation for a little boy who had just been sexually assaulted. I sat there on a wooden pallet with my arms wrapped around my knees, shivering in my shorts and bare feet. But for some strange reason, over the next several hours I felt that I was not alone in the cooler. I was too spiritually unaware to think about God or a heavenly presence, but I just knew that I was not alone. That thought – and death – was on my mind when I finally passed out.

I did not know that my family and neighbors had already begun a search for me. They initially thought that I had wandered down to a nearby pond, been bitten by a snake, or had drowned. Finally, after several hours of searching, someone said, "What if he got locked in the big cooler?" God must have put that thought into their heads. When they found me they rushed my unconscious body to the main house where I was wrapped in blankets and my feet were put in warm water. Eventually they set me on Grandma's front porch and aimed me toward the sun. Solar powered country medicine, I guess. It worked. Seems it wasn't my time to die yet.

When my cousins and other family members found out what had happened to me, they went after the child molester at his parents' house. First, they tore through the screen door and started to beat him mercilessly in front of his parents who did nothing. Then they tied his hands and feet and began to drag him behind a tractor. A rope was tossed over a limb as the child molester cried for mercy, "Please don't kill me! Please don't kill me!" The noose was tied around his neck and he was lifted off the ground. They let him swing until he passed out.

Thankfully they let him down before he died. Soon the child molester and his family moved away, and we never saw them again.

One of the toughest questions on earth is, "Where was God when I was [fill in the blank: raped, beaten, abandoned, dying, etc.]" How do you answer a question like that?

It's difficult, but five things I have learned:

1) Everything wicked comes from Satan.

2) Everything good comes from God.

3) Although God is powerful enough to do anything, He sometimes steps back and allows the bad consequences of sin to run their course on this broken planet.

4) The amazing thing is how God can bring good out of bad, like how springtime flowers come from the dry seeds that die in the autumn. He can "redeem" the bad things in your past so that you can go on to help others, just like God is allowing me to help others today – despite my past. I've been healed by Jesus.

5) There may be times in your life when bad things happen to you or someone you care about. Or you hear about something terrible like a natural or man-made disaster. Be careful not to blame God for bad things. Remember, oftentimes suffering is a consequence of a person or people's bad choices and God is not responsible for that. Remember, human nature in everyone is fallen. Our natural leaning is not toward God or doing good. Think about it: We have enough food and resources to keep kids and people from starving to death. We, as mankind, have the resources to provide clean drinking water and medicine that can provide good health for millions. But man is basically self-centered, greedy, and rebels against God. That is why we all need to trust and obey God so that we don't add to the negative consequences in this world. If you have asked God to forgive you and give you the power through His Holy Spirit to do right from this point on, He can, and you will!

"We know that all things work together for the good of those who love God – those whom He has called according to His plan."
– Romans 8:28

"The thief [Satan] comes only to steal, kill, and destroy. But I have come in order that you might have life – life in all its fullness!" – John 10:10 (GNB)

"...to console those who mourn in Zion, to give them beauty for ashes, the oil of joy for mourning, the garment of praise for the spirit of heaviness ..." – Isaiah 61:3 (NKJV)

chapter five

GROOMING AND GUARDIAN ANGELS

I was a mischievous kid who often sought recreation whenever and wherever I could find it. I would drop water balloons from a tree limb on passing cars. I would catch turtles and fish with a string and hook in the gully behind our house, or find girly magazines stashed in the bushes. One time a TV commercial for the Sunbeam Bread Company said that if anyone could find a dime-sized hole in a slice of their bread, they would give that person seven loaves of bread. I happened to find a tiny hole – much smaller than a dime – in a slice of bread one day. After carefully carving the hole bigger with a bobby pin, I showed it to the store down the street. A few days later a bread truck pulled up in front of our house and delivered seven loaves of bread. I thought that was cool, even though I knew it was wrong.

By the time I was in the first grade, I was shooting light bulbs out of the lamp posts with my slingshot – I even broke a car window once by mistake as it was passing my house. I was careless and reckless and too young and inexperienced about the ways of the world to realize that there would be consequences for my actions. Like the time I was running across the street with my friend without paying any attention to oncoming traffic. My friend was hit by a car and seriously injured. Both of his legs and one arm were broken.

When I was in grade school, I found an older friend who won my confidence. He was a young man who gave me the kind of attention that should come from a godly father. Obviously, I never had that kind of positive attention. This guy started taking me on fun trips away from home. He bought me toys and things. This went on for months and I thought it was pretty cool. What I didn't understand was that it was all a hoax. He was grooming me so that he could molest me. Then one day he said, "Hey Victor, let's do such-and-such." Something deep down inside of me knew that this was very wrong. But he said, "Come on – you can trust me. Look at all the stuff we've been doing together! Look at the special gifts I've given you. This is just between you and me. Nobody will know."

These people are called "groomers," and they're more common today than they were when I was a kid. The Internet has opened up so many more opportunities for boys and girls to be deceived and molested. Like I said, the worst part – and the thing that makes it so difficult to get out – is how they build up this false sense of trust and they make you feel like you're in it together. They even shift the blame onto your own back.

If that's happening to you, don't take it anymore! Run away and keep your boundaries up. No matter what you've done or what has been done to you, tell a parent or a teacher or a pastor or a law officer and get out now. You need to find somebody who can help you. Keep looking until you find someone who believes you.

Beware of groomers!

"Their lives are filled with all kinds of sexual sins, wickedness, and greed. They are mean. They are filled with envy, murder, quarreling, deceit, and viciousness. They are gossips, slanderers, haters of God, haughty, arrogant, and boastful. They think up new ways to be cruel." – Romans 1:29-30

"Stay away from such people. Some of these men go into homes and mislead weak-minded women..." [and children, I might add!] - 2 Timothy 3:5-6

I was ambushed, and I didn't know how to get out. So, he molested me, and the worst part was the guilt and shame I experienced for letting him do it. That really jacked my brain up, and it took me years to find healing from that shame. But I did eventually find healing. The one thing I'd tell you: When you've been molested, the shame is not yours, it's theirs!

Soon my family moved to Richburg Hills, Mississippi. My stepfather's drunkenness was causing all kinds of trouble. I remember one night when my parents got into a big fight out in the garage. It felt to me as if a cloud of evilness had invaded our home. My older brother, who was fourteen at the time, picked up my toy Davy Crockett long rifle, snapped it in two and went out to hit my dad with the wooden stock.

"Get away from my mom!" my brother shouted, waving the makeshift weapon in the air. "Leave her alone!"

I ran into the garage shaking with fear. I didn't see all that happened because my mother and brothers took me to bed and covered me with a blanket. Still I continued to shake violently. "Please make it stop!" I begged them. It took three or four hours before the shaking went away. My stepfather's alcoholic tirades were having a terrible effect on my family and me.

On another occasion he came home drunk and sat all the kids down on the couch. He interrogated each one of us about the whereabouts of one of his work tools. As we sat there he would say in a soft voice, "I'm going to whip each one of you unless someone tells me who took my hammer." My mother felt powerless to stop the terror. We never did find out what happened to that dang hammer.

It all ended one Saturday night when I was ten years old. My stepfather was working as a bail bondsman and he always carried a pistol. The indoor and outdoor house lights were on when my stepfather came home, and that's something he would not tolerate. He became enraged about all the energy we were wasting. He was angry and said the electric bill was too high, so he pulled out his gun and began shooting the outside lights. Bullets were flying everywhere. My mother rushed us into a closet, afraid that this would be our last night on earth.

Momma kept whispering, "Don't cry. Don't make a sound." Then she courageously stepped out of the closet and confronted my stepfather.

"Please don't do this," she said.

My stepfather screamed. "You kids come out of the closet!"

Then I heard my mother begin to pray fervently. "The blood of Jesus covers the door! The blood of Jesus covers the door!"

My stepfather tried to bully his way through the doorway, but at that moment an invisible wall stopped him cold at the threshold. He could not penetrate our sanctuary! We knew the Lord had posted a guardian angel at the doorway. After a few failed attempts to reach us, my stepfather gave up and walked away cussing and yelling. When he disappeared into his bedroom, Momma said to us, "We're gonna run." But my older sister Debbie was not home, and Momma had to warn her. Just then the telephone rang and so Momma ran to pick up the phone. Assuming it was my sister on the line, Momma shouted, "Debbie, don't come home!"

To my mother's horror it was not my sister but my stepfather. Sounding deep and demonic, he roared, "Rita, you come in our room now! We're gonna finish this now!" He was on the extension phone in the bedroom. Thinking fast Momma said, "Okay, but I need to go to the bathroom first." Then she hurried us out of the closet, telling us to be quiet. Momma opened a small window and one by one we all climbed out. We ran in the darkness to a neighbor's house where we were kept for the night.

When my oldest brother Tony came home after a weekend of hunting, all he found was a note saying we had moved. He had no clue where we went. So, he packed his clothes in his panel truck, drove into the woods, and set up a little camp down by the river. He finished his school year under those circumstances, hunting and fishing for food and doing odd jobs to make money. What a way to grow up! Tony was forced to become a man that year. No wonder he turned out to be one of the toughest karate and street fighters I have ever known. As for the rest of us, we hid out in the big city of Jackson for a while.

Can God really do those kinds of miracles? Can He block doorways and send angels to protect people? Well, I believe He can, because I've experienced that kind of protection so many times in my life. Look how God's Word says He gives special protection to "those who fear Him" and "to whose hearts are loyal to Him."

"The messenger of the LORD camps around those who fear Him, and He rescues them." – Psalm 34:7

"The Lord keeps close watch over the whole world to give strength to those whose hearts are loyal to Him." – 2 Chronicles 16:9 (GNB)

chapter six

STEALING AND DRINKING

My junior high school years were awful. My family lived in five different places. I attended four different schools and I was often bullied. I had two more stepfathers come into my life during these years. There were countless fights. My mother did her best to look out for me. My older brothers kept me out of trouble except for the times they led me into trouble, as teenage boys are prone to do. Our family was trying to survive the best we knew how.

In sixth grade we moved to Clinton, Mississippi, a small town near Jackson. We had so little money and my mother was working again, so I talked her into letting us take governmental food assistance at school. It was embarrassing at first, but my hunger was stronger than my pride. This was hard for Momma because she never wanted to depend on welfare. In order to convince her that I could use food stamps, I said, "Mom, you pay taxes, right? Well, all you're doing is getting back a little bit of your own money." It was a weak argument, but my mother bought it because she had no choice. That's how I ended up eating breakfast and lunch in the school cafeteria. With money being so tight, Momma made a lot of our food from scratch. I remember something she called "cush-cush." It was a Cajun type of cornbread baked in a big black skillet, and we would eat out of that pot for days.

In these tough times I began hanging out with some bad boys. I joined them in breaking into schools after hours and stealing stuff. We never got caught, which wasn't good for me because it only encouraged me to continue. I also got drunk for the first time before a football game. I stumbled onto the field and the school security dragged me off. I eventually wandered off and walked into a convenience store where a group of older kids began telling me I could fly. Pretty soon I was convinced that I could fly, so I went outside to leap over a truck.

"Victor!" somebody shouted.

A strong hand grabbed my shirt collar. My older brothers Tony and Mike had found me. They threw me into the back seat of the car and took me home. I staggered into our living room.

"You're drunk!" My mother blurted out.

"Yes, ma'am," I confessed.

My mother sat me down at the kitchen table and made me eat red beans and rice. In no time at all the room started spinning out of control and I threw up everything. I believe that's exactly what my Momma wanted to happen, because she really made me load up on those rice and beans. But it didn't stop me from getting deeper into alcohol in sixth grade … and marijuana too. My brothers were big pot smokers. I always heard my grandpa's voice in my head. He used to say, "Drinking is just what we do." So, I followed his advice. Meanwhile I was slowly sliding into a trap that had destroyed more men, women, and families than I could even begin to imagine.

One day my younger sister Chermayne spit on a neighborhood boy who was about my age. He retaliated by slapping her in the face. My brothers looked at the imprint of his hand on her cheek and they told me, "Victor, you'd better go beat the hell out of that boy." So, I walked to the kid's house across the street and knocked on the door, but he wouldn't come outside. I went back home and called him on the telephone, asking him to come over so we could talk. He made the mistake of believing me, so we met out in the front yard.

"Why did you slap my sister?" I asked.

"Because she spit on me," he replied. "And I just felt like it."

"Would you do it again?" I asked.

"Yeah," he said.

Before the word was out of his mouth I made him eat it by punching him in the face. Blood was flowing as he fell to the ground and started bawling. That's when my brothers who were watching started laughing their heads off! I jerked the boy to his feet and chased him home with more blows.

Unfortunately, this boy's sturdy German mother was a lot tougher and stronger than her boy. It wasn't long before my brothers were looking across the street with eyes as wide as saucers.

There's a great Bible verse that says:

"As a dog goes back to its vomit, so a fool repeats his stupidity."
– Proverbs 26:11

Genuine fools are people who reject the wisdom of God. That was me before I started applying the wisdom of God's Word (the Bible) to my life. You can see how I was becoming like that dog returning to the same old vomit.

Here's a tough question: In what area of life does it seem like you keep returning to the same bad choices or the same old sins? Did you know that God can help you change those habits? But you can't do it without Him. You must surrender your life to Him.

"So, I find that this law is at work: when I want to do what is good, what is evil is the only choice I have ... It makes me a prisoner to the law of sin which is at work in my body. What a miserable person I am! Who will rescue me from this body that is taking me to death? Thanks be to God, who does this through our Lord Jesus Christ! ... For the law of the Spirit, which brings us life in union with Christ Jesus, has set me free from the law of sin and death." – Romans 7:21 – 8:2 (GNB)

"Oh no, Victor," they said. "She's coming after you."

A muscular, thick-necked woman was charging across the street like a German panzer. As she attacked our front door with her fist, I quickly explained to my mother what had happened. Momma opened the door and scowled. Even though she was petite in comparison to this Bohemian Goliath, Momma had endured so much in life that she was not frightened in the least. She told this woman in no uncertain terms what had happened, and she ordered her off our property.

Now heed this warning – if you ever find yourself between this "momma bear" and her cubs ... you had better turn tail and run!

chapter seven

MY MOTHER STRIKES OUT AGAIN

As I began the seventh grade, my mother married her third husband. I hated this man with a vicious rage that seemed to eat away at me from the inside out. This man had just gotten out of the Navy where he had been a cook. He owned a restaurant and a drive-thru liquor store called the "Beer Barn" in Jackson. People would order their alcohol from a drive-through window without having to get out of the car. I was sure my mother married him for his money.

This guy wasted no time in putting me to work at his restaurant bussing tables, mopping, cleaning bathrooms, and doing dishes. He also taught me how to cook, use the cash register, and close the books. Since he was my legal guardian he had the authority to take me out of school to work and he did this consistently. In time his behavior grew more and more irrational. He put a chain on our freezer at home, so we couldn't "steal" any food. He pulled the spark plug wires off our cars, so we couldn't drive. After just three months of marriage my mother finally announced, "Kids, we're outta here!"

My oldest brother who was employed at the Beer Barn must have thought he deserved a bonus before he quit working for our stepfather. He called all his friends on the phone and said, "Boys. There's a special tonight at the Beer Barn. Come load up!" After they had taken what they wanted, my brothers packed up their own vehicle with beer and drove to another state. The rest of the family moved back to Jackson.

When I entered the eighth grade at another school, my mother met and married another man. He was a commercial diver for one of the largest oil companies on the Gulf of Mexico. He was a quiet man – part Native

American – and he had no children. I liked him, and I eventually grew to love and trust him as much as I could. He would sometimes be gone for weeks at a time while he did saturation dives for oil companies. He would go underwater and stay in a submersible bubble for thirty days, making a thousand dollars a day. Oxygen and gases were properly mixed, so he could breathe – now this was dangerous work! Our lives were much better off with this man. He made us feel somewhat secure and settled, which we desperately needed.

I wish I'd known about bitterness and unforgiveness many years ago. It's like drinking a poison and hoping it will hurt someone else. You might go out to hurt that other person, but nobody gets hurt worse than you in the end. How do you get free from that kind of bitterness? Only God can remove it. And it helps to talk with a Christian counselor or friend about it, because they can help keep you on the right path. And remember that each one of us is sinful and rebellious and in need of God's forgiveness. Not one of us is perfect.

"If you forgive others the wrongs they have done to you, your Father in heaven will also forgive you. But if you do not forgive others, then your Father will not forgive the wrongs you have done." – Matthew 6:14-15 (GNB)

"Be tolerant with one another and forgive one another whenever any of you has a complaint against someone else. You must forgive one another just as the Lord has forgiven you." – Colossians 3:13 (GNB)

"I will purify them from the sins that they have committed against me, and I will forgive their sins and their rebellion."–Jeremiah 33:8 (GNB)

When I was a kid, it was always just when you thought everything was fine that the weird stuff started to happen again. I have a horrible memory during this time of a teenage friend who killed herself with a shotgun. My mind flashes back to the police taking me to her apartment and bringing me upstairs to view the blood-stained floor and walls. Or I remember our sweet neighbor lady who was abducted, raped, and later found in a field brutally murdered.

I'll never forget one night when I was awakened by a drunken "friend of the family" who was trying to molest me. I freaked out and went ape crazy by grabbing a 2x4 piece of wood from the garage. Then I commenced with the intention to beat the hell out him. When my older brother Mike walked in and found out what had happened, he took a turn and started beating on the punk. Then Mike dumped his bashed-up body outside the guy's own house in the wee hours of the morning. This kind of junk was becoming a "normal" part of childhood for me. Sick, isn't it?

chapter eight

Dipping Tobacco and Slaying Suitors

When I was fourteen, I told my latest stepfather that I wanted to start dipping. He thought a moment and then softly replied, "Okay. I'll be right back." He bought me a can of Copenhagen tobacco and left me with this challenge: "See if you can dip the whole can."

I didn't know any better, so I walked outside, sat down on a stump, opened the can, and put some tobacco in my mouth. After chewing and spitting a while, I took some more. And some more. I dipped and dipped until half the can was gone. The only reason I stopped is because the whole world started spinning. I watched my stepfather climb over the edge of that spinning horizon with a big fat grin on his face.

"Looks like you're gonna be sick, boy."

And I was. It was so bad that I never dipped again for the rest of my life. My stepfather had done me a big favor, one that I greatly appreciate.

Moving was as predictable for our family as Christmas or Independence Day. In the middle of my eighth grade we moved to West Lake, Louisiana, because my grandmother and her husband E.J. lived there. E.J. was a tattooed old sailor and one of the meanest men who ever lived. And I don't mean that as a compliment.

West Lake was a smelly polluted town full of oil refineries. I got bullied a lot in school. I also fought with my sister Debbie, but that was a losing proposition because the rule in our family was that girls could hit a boy, but the boy couldn't hit back. Debbie began dating a guy named Bo who was about nineteen and a drug user and a punk thug. My sister did what most girls who have never known the love and security of a caring father did. She turned to a guy who gave her the wrong kind of "love and affection" that had all kinds of strings attached.

I didn't know much about true love either, but I knew that I hated Bo. So, one day I climbed on the roof of our house with a pellet gun and pumped it up to its maximum pressure. Then I lay in wait for him and his brother Poodle who lived two houses down from us. When they got within range, I put my sights on the middle of Bo's back and squeezed the trigger. He jumped up and down and began screaming like he'd been stung by a hornet. He fell on the ground and began thrashing about. I shimmied off my roof, slipped inside my house and acted as if nothing had ever happened.

Several days later I climbed back on my roof and shot at them again. Two weeks after that I did it again. The best thing about it was that I never got caught. Looking back, I see that kind of stuff as a sick way to vent all the anger that was pent up inside of me.

One day, things got crazy and fast while I was in a heated argument with my sister Debbie. I grabbed a knife, but she wrenched it away from me and threatened to cut me. So, I slammed her against a wall and bear-hugged her until her arms went limp and she dropped the knife.

"You're never gonna stab me," I told her. She said the exact same thing to me. That was the last time we ever fought.

Bo gave Debbie an engagement ring, but that's when my petite little momma became that growling momma bear again.

"It ain't gonna happen," she told Debbie. She didn't want her girl making the same mistakes that she had made. This irritated Bo's mother and sister greatly. One of them made the mistake of coming over to our house talking trash and making threats and confronting my mother. Again, Mother went ballistic like she was protecting her little cub. I literally had to hold her back to keep her off of that woman. By now you know my mother was a scrapper. There was no doubt about that. It didn't make sense that my mother would constantly put us in dangerous positions then fight with all her might to get us out of them. But it was true. She was simply doing her best with the skills that had been handed down to her.

Later Bo showed up at our door, shouting, "I want Debbie! I want Debbie!" My stepfather opened the door and quietly said, "You need to go on home now, son."

Bo answered defiantly, "I ain't going home without Debbie."

My stepfather attempted to shut the door, but Bo stuck his foot out and stopped him.

"I'm telling you to go home," my stepfather repeated.

"I ain't leaving without her!" Bo screamed as he tried to force his way into our house.

My stepfather grabbed Bo by the shirt and said, "You want to be a man? Then this is how we do it." Right there in that doorway I saw the Indian warrior in my stepfather erupt. He tore that punk up right there. It was like, beat him down, knock him into tomorrow, show him where he don't belong! The whole family was impressed by my stepfather's show of force. It would be a while before I learned just how deadly this man could be. Well, it is safe to say that Bo and Debbie's hopes for marriage ended on that doorstep.

I guess we're all products of our upbringing more than we realize. Like they say, "The apple doesn't fall very far from the tree." We are all members of the same sinful human family. We all have been deceived by Satan. Nothing the world has to offer will ever give us true satisfaction. Only Jesus can bring lasting happiness and satisfaction.

"Everything leads to weariness– a weariness too great for words. Our eyes can never see enough to be satisfied; our ears can never hear enough ... I decided to enjoy myself and find out what happiness is. But I found that this is useless too ... If you love money, you will never be satisfied; if you long to be rich, you will never get all you want. It is useless." – Ecclesiastes 1:8, 2:1, 5:10 (GNB)

"The thief [Satan] comes only to steal, kill, and destroy. But I [Jesus] have come in order that you might have life – life in all its fullness!" – John 10:10 (GNB)

"You prepare a banquet for me while my enemies watch. You anoint my head with oil. My cup overflows. Certainly, goodness and mercy will stay close to me all the days of my life, and I will remain in the Lord's house for days without end." – Psalm 23:5-6

chapter nine

TRUMPETS AND SWAMPS

In eighth grade, I was a skinny eighty-five pounds with big feet and a concave hole in my chest. I wasn't any good at athletics, but I sure excelled at being a poor student. I can joke about that today, but at that time I had no self-esteem. Well, maybe some. On a scale of one to ten my self-esteem was about negative six. I felt totally worthless. Eighth grade was actually the hardest year of my life and that's saying a lot considering my previous years. I hid my despair behind a happy façade.

For some unknown reason girls liked to talk to me, but even that led to conflict with other boys who were jealous of the attention I received. One day a group of bullies cornered me in the locker room and I tried to fight my way out. They overpowered me, lifted me up, spread my feet wide, carried me over to a pole, held one leg on each side and slammed me groin-first into the pole. It's difficult to describe that kind of a feeling. I thought perhaps that an atom bomb had just exploded. They dropped me to the floor and I curled into a ball. The excruciating pain had not even faded before I was planning my revenge.

Someday I'm going to pay them back.

I was desperate and depressed, so I arranged a visit with the school counselor. I wanted to talk to a counselor about what had just happened. Then she walked into the room. She greeted me cordially and asked how she could help me. I could not bring myself to talk. I simply started sobbing uncontrollably. It was a dam of shame, guilt, anger that burst forth. She did the wisest thing: just let me sit there and cry. What could I say about my experience in the locker room and what was happening in my life? I was tongue-tied. I was an emotional wreck. I wish I could've put my anger and emotions into words to her that day, but I never knew how to communicate my feelings. But I am glad that I utilized my God-given gift: my tear ducts.

Everybody wants to know they are worth something, right? Well, I felt pretty worthless. Maybe you know the feeling. That's what drives so many young people to depression and suicide and destructive behavior.

If there's one message I'd like to personally deliver to every troubled kid in the world today, it's this: Somebody loves you more than you will ever know. That Somebody is Jesus. He loves us so much that He died a brutal death on the cross to pay the punishment that you and I deserve. Read this Bible verse and plug your name into the blanks.

This is how much God loves you: "God so loved [your name] that He gave His one and only Son, so that if [you] believe in Him, [you] need not die but have eternal life." – John 3:16

This is God's gift of love for you! And that's not all. Many followers of Jesus here on earth love you too. I found them after I gave my life to Jesus. You can find them too! I want you to know that you are an awesome gift from God!

After eighth grade I transitioned to West Lake High School where I would start my third year of playing the trumpet in the school band. I thought I was pretty good, but out of three sections, I was placed in the last chair of the last section. That left me dead last in a group of twenty-seven trumpet players, despite the fact that I loved playing trumpet and I practiced up to five hours a day at home.

One day the band director held a competition in which we could challenge the person in the chair next to us. Both musicians would play the same music and the better player moved up or kept the higher chair. So, I began challenging people up my row and I ended up beating everyone in the third section. None of these players knew me, and they couldn't believe what was happening. Next, I went to challenge the players in the second section. Within a short time, I had wiped out everyone in that section too.

The band room became real tense, as if it were a big championship game. They were probably thinking, *who is this skinny, blonde, feather-haired kid?* They didn't know that I played along with Maynard Ferguson record albums at home. My older brother Mike was awesome on the horn and I simply followed his example.

Then I began my assault on the first section. When this little freshman started whipping all the seniors in the first row, the place was going wild. I was putting on a real show and I kept it going right up to the very first guy in the very first chair. I don't remember his name, but he had red hair, buck teeth, and a little mustache. He was kind of a nerd. I sat down next to him and stared straight right into his face. He looked red-faced and scared. The proper etiquette was to say, "I challenge you," which I had said twenty-five times that day. Instead this time I said, "Do you want me to challenge you?"

"No," he answered, knowing that if I beat him then he was no longer the number one reigning trumpet player.

I smiled. "Well, I'm not going to challenge you."

There was a gasp in the room. People could not believe what I had said. They knew I was better than that guy and he knew it too. But the reason I didn't challenge him was that he was the only person who had introduced himself and befriended me when I walked into that school weeks earlier. The only person that did. That's why I chose to honor him that day. And for the first time in my life, I had succeeded in something that made me feel good about myself.

I felt great about my decision to leave that senior classman in the first-place chair. Jesus said, "Blessed are those who are meek" (Matthew 5:5), and meekness is best defined as power under control. What I learned was that just because I had the power to beat this guy didn't mean that I had to beat him. Knowing that I could beat him was good enough for me. Hopefully that will encourage you to have mercy on other people and honor them rather than try to prove that you are better than them.

Sometimes when you put another's needs before your own, you also get a great deal!

At that time my mother had a beauty shop called "La Place." The shop was in Lake Charles, so we had to drive across a long, dangerously high bridge to get there. Many accidents occurred there. It gave me quite a scare and my Catholic MawMaw made the sign of the cross each time she traveled over the bridge.

I experienced some real adventures in West Lake. We lived on the bayou and adjacent some mean water moccasins. I would shoot at their heads and some of them were so mean they would come out of the water after me! I also set fishing lines to catch catfish. One day I was in the back of our boat and my stepfather sat in the front at the controls. All of a sudden, he gunned the engine and a hook on the trout line went deep into my finger. I screamed my head off, so he stopped the boat just in time before the line attached to the hook ran out. It probably would have pulled the hook all the way through. We dug out the hook and my finger bled like a stuck pig.

On another moonlit night, a friend and I climbed into a yellow canoe to explore the swamp. We were telling jokes and laughing, and then I rocked the boat so far that it accidentally tipped over. Both of us fell into the swamp, which is a scary thing in the broad daylight, but it was horrifying at night. I knew there were snakes there, along with one really big alligator. My friend managed to scurry back into the canoe and I found myself standing in waist-deep water. As I lunged for the canoe I stepped into a hole and went beneath the surface. The thing that scared me to death was that I knew I had stepped into an alligator den. They hide in those holes underwater.

Now in case you didn't know, there's one thing you want to avoid more than anything. It's being sucked into an alligator hole in the swamp in the black of night. I went crazy, screaming like a madman. I frantically kicked my way up, beating the water with my paddle. Somehow, I fell into the canoe like a soaking wet swamp rat, my heart pumping bullets. Then I told my buddy that I would never go into the swamp at night again. Ever. We laughed it off and headed for dry land.

chapter ten

THE ANGER YEARS

Before my freshman year ended, I got revenge on a dude who was always pushing and hitting and bullying me. He was one of the fellows who slid me on that pole in the locker room the year before. He had come to expect that I'd passively take whatever he dished out. Then one day I surprised him by turning on him like a chainsaw. I beat the tar out of him, right in front of all the kids who were walking to their buses. He kept screaming as I hammered him about the head and shoulders. That bully never picked on me again. In fact, no one else did either, at least not without me fighting back.

The rest of my high school years made some of my junior high days look like a Sunday school picnic. There were times when I hit rock bottom and then there were days when I could have been mistaken for an angelic choirboy. I had days of darkness and days of light. Some people said, "Victor's a rebel – a first-class troublemaker." But sometimes I showed real promise. And the girls seemed to like me, so that helped. Even when I didn't ask for it, it seemed as if trouble followed me, like I was cursed by that dead, black cat put on my head as a child. One innocent job as a stock boy at a little country store in DeRidder turned sour. The owner accused me of getting fresh with his daughter and he fired me. I told him he was wrong, and I held no inappropriate affection for his daughter. Later I learned that he himself was the one messing with her.

As you can see, I was an extremely angry, frustrated, troubled boy. A lot of that came from when I was molested and abandoned and humiliated and beaten. The unfortunate fact of life is that every human being experiences the good and the bad. The question is – how do we respond to the bad?

> *Look at it this way - basically we can travel only two roads in life. One leads to eternal life. The other leads to eternal death. One finds joy in loving others and doing good. The other becomes bitter by hurting others and by following sinful, destructive desires. One leads to God and an eternal family. The other leads to Satan and a lonely hell. It's easy to think you don't have a choice in life when bad things in your past happened without your choice. But you can't keep blaming others for the bad things that happened to you. Jesus can heal your wounds, but often the scars can remain as a reminder of how merciful Jesus is to love and heal your hurts. You can choose to let Jesus heal your past. You choose the road to life and to healing – it is not chosen by your parents or your abusers or by anyone else. I hope and pray that you choose the road to life.*
>
> *"Choose today whom you will serve ... My family and I will still serve the Lord." –Joshua 24:15*

In the tenth grade, I was gangly, and I shot up to a whole one hundred and five pounds. I had braces on my teeth. I parted my long, blonde hair down the middle and combed it back. Like many teens I also had terminal acne. I attended two schools as a sophomore: Moss Bluff High School and – are you ready for this – Alleluia Acres. AA was a Christian school that my three sisters and I entered about two-thirds of the way into the school year. Because of my acting up, Momma thought the Christian school would do me some good. The temptations at the public school were too great for me. My drug habits and drinking and carousing were getting out of control, so Momma decided to seize the moment and do something about it. Unfortunately, Alleluia Acres was a small school and the administrators weren't ready for somebody like me. I eventually tried to get some of the Christian boys to use drugs. Without a doubt I was a rotten apple in the barrel from day one.

I introduced the boys to drag racing. I had a little Datsun truck and I convinced my new buddies to skip school and race around town with me. The principal called Momma at her work and told her the bad news. That really upset her. So, Momma called my stepfather at home and he became livid. When I got home that afternoon he really lashed out at me.

"Your mother is angry and I'm gonna have to whip you!"

He went into his woodshop and carved a paddle out of a two-by-four.

Then he spanked me. Suddenly my temper flared, and I turned, wanting to hit him. But he saw it coming and I was forced to stop short, with my fists clenched tight as hammer anvils, wanting to swing.

"Okay," he said. "Next time we'll fight like men with our fists. No paddle."

Then he walked into a back room and slid an old briefcase from beneath his bed. "I've never showed you these before, but I think it's time now." He opened the briefcase and took out some yellowed newspaper clippings. "Read them." A newspaper photo depicted a handcuffed, wild-looking biker dude with long hair standing before a judge. The accompanying article stated that the biker was from Arizona and had gotten into a bar fight years earlier. He had shot two men, killed one, and been convicted of murder. It was only then that I realized the story was about my stepfather. This soft-spoken man had spent time in Chino Prison in California, one of the toughest prisons in America.

"Blessed are those who endure when they are tested. When they pass the test, they will receive the crown of life that God has promised to those who love Him. When someone is tempted, he shouldn't say that God is tempting him. God can't be tempted by evil, and God doesn't tempt anyone. Everyone is tempted by his own desires as they lure him away and trap him. Then desire becomes pregnant and gives birth to sin. When sin grows up, it gives birth to death.
"My dear brothers and sisters don't be fooled. Every good present and every perfect gift comes from above, from the Father who made the sun, moon, and stars." – James 1:12-19

I later learned that he had been released early because he qualified as a commercial diver in a program similar to the Navy SEALS. His skills somehow allowed him to get out of prison early. The authorities actually didn't think he would survive the course, but my stepfather did. That's how he ended up becoming a commercial diver. After reading the clippings I knew I'd better not skip school anymore. My stepfather's past scared me straight – for the time - and so I tried to make things work at Alleluia Acres.

chapter eleven

HEARING GOD'S VOICE

When my sisters and I enrolled at Alleluia Acres we also began attending the church by the same name. Dr. Mike Clark was our pastor, principal, and coach. He was one of the first Christians I had ever met, and he really influenced me in a positive way. He showed amazing compassion and patience for us kids, especially considering all the headaches I must have given him. Like most kids I could spot a phony a mile away, but Dr. Mike Clark was the real deal. He not only talked the talk of a Christian, but he walked the walk.

One day a visiting evangelist came to our church to preach. The small church was packed with attendees for the service that day. As the man preached, he suddenly pointed straight at me and said, "God wants you to know something!" Then he motioned for me to come up front. I didn't want to go but I was too scared to run.

When I arrived at the front of the church the preacher said, "God wants you to know He's going to use you in a mighty way. God's going to use you to be a mighty man for His glory. You're going to be used as a rod of love to keep people from destroying themselves. God wants you to know that He's got plans for you ... big plans." It was as though God Himself was telling me, "I am going to use your manliness as a heavenly tool to help troubled people keep from destroying themselves." My first thoughts were, "You got to be nuts! Manliness? I'm a weak, skinny kid. Help people? I can't even help myself!"

Do you believe in "chance" or "coincidence?" Was it just chance that led me to Alleluia Acres? Did that preacher pick me out of the crowd and prophesy over me because of "chance?" Is it by "coincidence" that you've picked up this book? Is it "chance" that's leading you to think about spiritual things today? Sorry, but I don't believe in chance. God has His sights on you. He's been speaking to you. He's sent people into your life to lead you closer to Him. You know the words He's been whispering in your ear. "There's got to be more to life than this. There must be something better than eating, drinking, getting high, and using people. There must be true love somewhere – there must be somebody who truly cares."

This is what he actually said! But at the time I was definitely not ready to receive that word from God. I went back to my pew knowing the preacher had simply picked out the wrong guy. I could barely keep from destroying myself – how could I possibly help other people? I called myself a Christian, but I lived like the worst sinner. I never read the Bible or had any interest in the things pertaining to the Lord. That's how I saw myself. That's how I expected things to remain. But thankfully that wasn't the destiny God had in store for me. Little did I know that my aimless wandering through the wilderness would eventually lead me to an incredible Promised Land. But first I had some more wandering to do.

That is the voice of God and He's calling you today. He is True Love! Will you listen to Him? Will you accept His wonderfully healing plan for your life?

"I know the plans that I have for you, declares the Lord. They are plans for peace and not disaster, plans to give you a future filled with hope." – Jeremiah 29:11

"This is what I do: I don't look back, I lengthen my stride, and I run straight toward the goal to win the prize that God's heavenly call offers in Christ Jesus." – Philippians 3:13-14

chapter twelve

RADIO WAVES AND WHIRLPOOLS

A couple of my friends helped me get a really interesting job at a Christian radio station. I worked the midnight to six A.M. shift as a disc jockey, even though I had no prior experience. The radio technicians taught me how to run the controls, play music, and air the commercials. I even learned how to take news and weather reports from the Associated Press machine. I was extremely motivated to learn so I picked up everything quickly. On one of my shifts I was tired, and I needed a rest. I put on a record that lasted twenty-two minutes and I set my wristwatch alarm for the same time. Within a minute I was sound asleep. I awoke to the banging of a police officer on the station window.

"Are you all right, boy?" he asked. I jumped to attention. "Yes, sir."

"Well, that record you're playin' has been goin' bump-bump-bump for twenty minutes," the officer told me. "I got worried and came by to check on you." Fortunately, I didn't lose my job that night.

During the summer after my sophomore year, my parents sent me to stay with a couple of their friends in Texas for two weeks. The man was a commercial diver like my stepfather. He had a really nice black Corvette that he let me drive even though I was only fifteen.

The cool thing I've learned about God is that He's not a mean old man who slaps you with a stick whenever you sin. The Bible says He's a God of love. (1 John 4:8) He's patient and kind and forgiving. That doesn't mean we should sin all we can – He's clever and He knows when people are trying to manipulate Him and use His forgiveness as an excuse to sin. (Romans 6:1-2) He is compassionate and loving, and He's ready to forgive everyone who is truly sorry for their sins. Have you asked Him to forgive you and change your life? He's waiting for you, like a loving Father.

"He is the one who forgives all your sins, the one who heals all your diseases." – Psalm 103:3

"God is faithful and reliable. If we confess our sins, He forgives them and cleanses us from everything we've done wrong." –1 John 1:9

After a few days there the guy asked me, "Hey, you wanna get high?" I had stopped taking drugs and alcohol since I was attending a Christian school and was working at a Christian radio station. Several months of positive Christian influence had actually begun to turn my life around. But I was weak, and I eventually gave in to temptation and started using drugs again. I felt betrayed by my parents for sending me to stay with this man and his girlfriend, and I was sickened by my slide back into evil. I felt like a miserable failure.

About that time, my Uncle Larry was fishing in Florida when his boat came loose from the dock and drifted away. Larry jumped into the water to catch it. Meanwhile the wind blew the boat farther and farther away. By the time Larry realized that he couldn't catch the boat all of his strength was gone. He never made it back to shore. Larry was my mother's third brother to die unexpectedly. My family was brokenhearted. Larry was a good man and we all felt a deep sense of loss at his death. Once again, I felt God had played a cruel, evil joke by allowing my uncle to die. He was the closest male role model I had and the only one I had come to trust and now he was gone.

chapter thirteen

YOYO CHRISTIANITY

My brief radio experience motivated me to try my hand in the television industry. TV had a certain glamour that appealed to me. In Lake Charles there was an NBC television affiliate known as KPLC- TV. So, in eleventh grade I drove to the station to apply for a job.

"You're too young," I was told. "We don't have any positions for kids your age."

"I can do your audio work if you just give me a chance," I blurted out.

"Son, we appreciate your enthusiasm, but it's just not going to happen."

I refused to give up. I kept driving back to that television station until I ended up in front of the station general manager. I made them an offer that I thought they couldn't refuse.

"If you just give me a chance I'll work for free," I offered.

The general manager sent me to the human resources department where a man looked at me and said, "Victor, we're going to hire you. You'll be making $3.25 an hour, which is minimum wage."

I was initially hired as an audio operator trainee. My job was to monitor sounds of television programs and the microphone levels of the newscasters. I would also play the background music to sports videos and bloopers. My schedule was fixed so I could leave school in the early afternoon to work at the station until 10:30 at night. I was nicknamed "The Kid" by the people at the station. I was taught to work behind the cameras and write copy for the news people. Later I became a technical director and I even learned to run the controls. On some days I would actually turn the station on and play the national anthem. For the first time in my life I realized I had the skills to do an important job. I was trusted and valued. This meant a lot to me considering all my self-esteem issues. What I would ultimately learn is it was not about self-esteem but, believe it or not, Christ-esteem. Wanting and esteeming Christ more than myself would be a secret key to my life, especially real joy. But it would not be learned yet.

Things were looking up for me, but sunny skies soon turned dark. It began with a hopeful friendship. You'd think I'd be more careful with relationships, after all my encounters with freaks who wanted to mess up my life. But I wasn't. You see there was a guy at the television station who I really admired. He was just out of college – a really smart and super cool guy. He had plenty of money and he drove a cherry Trans-Am that was out of this world. Well he started to take me under his wing, so I pulled away from my Christian high school buddies. He was letting me drive his car and this was too cool for words! However, he soon was giving me drugs and I was using again! Like a dog going back to his vomit!

One weekend he invited me to go to a beach party in another state, and I was like, "Yeah! Let's do it!" There'd be plenty of drugs and women and so-called good times. So, we loaded up the car and he picked up this other guy to go with us. We had a pretty wild time, but things went seriously crazy when they laced my drink with a paralyzing drug. I remember being barely conscious in an alley, lying between some garbage cans. They dragged me to a motel room, and in my moments of consciousness I remember my TV station "friend" breathing in my face, asking me if I could hear him.

I never put myself in a situation like that again. We all do stupid stuff, but the key is don't get stuck in a cycle of stupidity.

Thankfully I walked away from that experience and lived to tell you about it. Other people have not been so lucky. Unfortunately, horrible things happen to people all the time. Girls are especially vulnerable, but it happens to boys as well. My strongest word of advice is to keep your distance from people you don't trust. Beware of groomers like this man who try to gain your trust, so they can ambush you.

How do you know if you're headed for trouble? Well you could start by staying away from the obvious things like drugs and alcohol and sex outside of marriage, or any kind of activity that God's Word, the Bible, warns us to avoid. That would have certainly kept me out of trouble. What's more, listen to those little warnings in your heart. If something subtle makes you feel uncomfortable about someone, then get away. That's better than ending up where I did – or worse, dead on the pavement beside some dirty old trash cans.

"You must understand this: In the last days there will be violent periods of time. People will be selfish and love money. They will brag, be arrogant, and use abusive language. They will curse their parents, show no gratitude, have no respect for what is holy, and lack normal affection for their families. They will refuse to make peace with anyone. They will be slanderous, lack self-control, be brutal, and have no love for what is good. They will be traitors. They will be reckless and conceited. They will love pleasure rather than God. They will appear to have a godly life, but they will not let its power change them. Stay away from such people. Some of these men go into homes and mislead weak-minded women who are burdened with sins and led by all kinds of desires." – 2 Timothy 3:1-6

"What human nature does is quite plain. It shows itself in immoral, filthy, and indecent actions; in worship of idols and witchcraft. People become enemies and they fight; they become jealous, angry, and ambitious. They separate into parties and groups; they are envious, get drunk, have orgies, and do other things like these. I warn you now as I have before: those who do these things will not possess the Kingdom of God. But the Spirit produces love, joy, peace, patience, kindness, goodness, faithfulness, humility, and self-control. There is no law against such things as these. And those who belong to Christ Jesus have put to death their human nature with all its passions and desires." – Galatians 5:19- 24 (GNB)

After that I completed my junior year at Alleluia Acres. There was no band at AA, but they did have a music program that allowed me to compete at regional and state levels. I moved up through regionals playing trumpet and then competed in the state championship. What an amazing day it was when they awarded me the blue ribbon! That year I became Louisiana State's champion trumpet player. Then I advanced to the national competition in Dallas. I didn't win the nationals but that was okay with me, because I had a lot of fun and enjoyed the competition.

On the trip to Dallas my family passed through Jasper, Texas. "This is so pretty," my parents exclaimed. They toured the area and on the spur of the moment they decided to move there. I had only one year of high school left and we were moving again. Darn! I would have to give up my job at the television station, which greatly disappointed me. So, we moved that summer and I met a family that owned a Brahma bull ranch. They were good Christian people and thankfully they let me work on their ranch. I liked them because their lifestyle encouraged me to live in a way that was pleasing to God. Not only that, but this man and woman showed me what a good Christian marriage could look like … in the deepest part of me, I wanted to have a good job and a good marriage where love and respect were normal… and I actually began to imagine I could have a healthy relationship like theirs someday. It sure looked good to me!

chapter fourteen

JAIL TIME

Jasper High School became the fourteenth school I attended. I was now living with my two younger sisters and my parents. My stepfather continued his job as a commercial diver in the Gulf of Mexico. Unfortunately, I was not well received by the boys in my class. I was wearing my Calvin Klein jeans one day when a classmate approached me. "I bet you don't even have a pair of Wranglers in your closet, do ya?" he said in his Texas drawl. I didn't, but in a few days, I made sure I had a pair.

There were about six hundred students in my high school and I enjoyed playing trumpet in the school band. I played lots of solos in the marching band, and I joined the symphonic band too. I was accepted into the speech and drama club, which paved the way for me to begin acting in school plays. Later I worked my way up to president of the club. "All right!" I thought. "I'm doing pretty well for my first year here!"

Everybody has different opinions of what is right and wrong. How does God expect His children to behave? He says that we should be "holy" and "righteous," which means obeying His instructions in the Bible. He expects us to behave better than people who don't serve God – for His glory, but also for our own protection because every sin will hurt us in the end. As we saw earlier, He is loving and ready to forgive us when we fail. Still, He expects us to be faithful to Him, in the same way that husbands and wives should be faithful to each other. We cannot love both God and the world.

"No one can serve two masters." – Matthew 6:24

A community theatre group was putting on the musical Oklahoma, so I tried out and got the part of the Peddler. I wore a cowboy outfit and appeared in two or three shows every weekend for a while. Since I had now grown taller I tried out for the basketball team, but I was out of shape and I didn't make the cuts. Once again, I fell in with a bad crowd who liked to get drunk and party. I had been doing a pretty good job staying off drugs until I met a man who liked chasing high school girls and eating dried mushrooms. Once again temptation got the best of me and I joined him in getting loaded. This guy almost shot me with a shotgun when I unexpectedly showed up at his house one night. Bad timing – he was hiding from the enraged father of one of the girls he had gotten tangled up with.

One night I got arrested at a wild party by a Texas Highway Patrolman. He cuffed me and hauled me to the local town jail. I continued to run my mouth until I got worked by a nightstick a few times. After that I was given the "One Phone Call" in which I called my mom.

"Momma, the police have me locked up at the station and they beat me with a night stick!" I explained. The phone line went dead. My mother had hung up on me! Nobody came to my rescue, so I spent the night in jail. My mother showed up the next day. She didn't hurry getting there so I would have time to think about the consequences of my actions.

Maybe that's why I never went back to jail again.

"You are chosen people, a royal priesthood, a holy nation, people who belong to God. You were chosen to tell about the excellent qualities of God, who called you out of darkness into His marvelous light. Once you were not God's people, but now you are. Once you were not shown mercy, but now you have been shown mercy. Dear friends, since you are foreigners and temporary residents in the world, I'm encouraging you to keep away from the desires of your corrupt nature. These desires constantly attack you. Live decent lives among unbelievers." – 1 Peter 2:9-12

In case you think you are too weak to fight temptation on your own strength – you are right! But don't fret. As you get closer to Jesus and as you deepen your relationship with Him, He gives you strength to overcome all of the Devil's temptations.

"My grace is all you need, for my power is greatest when you are weak." – 2 Corinthians 12:9 (GNB)

"Trust the Lord with all your heart, and do not rely on your own understanding. In all your ways acknowledge Him and He will make your paths smooth." -Proverbs 3:5

chapter fifteen

GOD HAS GOOD EYESIGHT

Those days I wasn't watching God too closely, but I believe He never took His eyes off of me. Remember that message from God I received from the evangelist in Louisiana? Well, I got a second message from the Lord at a little Pentecostal church in Texas called Life Tabernacle. I was playing the drums in the praise band, but I lived the life of a hypocrite who partied every Saturday night and then tried to look holy on Sunday mornings. One Sunday I showed up at church completely hung over. Somehow, I managed to play all the songs.

In the middle of worship, the pastor's wife got a word from the Lord for me. She called me out from behind the drum set and said, "Victor ... would you please come here?"

I walked over, somehow expecting her to tell everyone about my immoral lifestyle.

"Victor," she said, "God wants you to know He's going to use you in a mighty way. You're going to be a mighty man of God for His kingdom. You're going to be a rod of love to keep people from ruining their lives."

"When you pray, don't be like hypocrites. They like to stand in synagogues and on street corners to pray so that everyone can see them. I can guarantee this truth: That will be their only reward." – Matthew 6:5

"They claim to know God, but they deny Him by what they do. They are detestable, disobedient, and unfit to do anything good." – Titus 1:16

Although God never stopped loving me, He sure didn't like my sin of hypocrisy – playing in the worship band at church while getting loaded with my friends. Who are we trying to fool when we act so holy in front of people while living a lie? God says that is "detestable." It obviously shows that we care more about the opinion of people than we do about God who sees right through our little act.

Then she smiled. "Has anyone ever spoken to you like this before?"

I was completely stunned by her words. I remembered the evangelist from the Alleluia service two years earlier. I thought about my momma who often said, "Victor, God's got a call on your life." What do you do with those messages from God when you're living about as far away from Him as you can get? Either you believe the words and start walking into the destiny that God has prepared for you ... or you pretend like you never heard anything. Regretfully, I chose the latter route.

I never returned to Life Tabernacle. I was afraid that I could not live up to the expectations that these people had placed on me. I couldn't get my mind around the fact that I had a purpose or any value in God's eyes. So, I rebelled against God and against the goodness that others saw in me. I would smoke pot before school and enter first period stoned. One night I broke into a school bus and vandalized it. Another time I broke into a teacher's locker and stole the mid-term exam. I went to the library and photocopied fifty copies, then returned the original to the teacher's locker. I sold copies of the midterm for ten dollars each. When finals rolled around I broke into the same teacher's locker and did it again. On the day of the finals I looked at the test, and immediately I realized that the questions had been changed. The teacher gave me a sly look and that's when I knew I wasn't as smart as I thought.

I assumed that was the end of my trouble with the high school authorities, until the day of my graduation. The teachers and staff wanted to make sure that no one sneaked any air horns or "disruptive devices" into the gymnasium to disturb the graduation ceremony so they had all the "rowdy seniors" line up one-by-one and get checked.

When it came to my turn to be checked, a coach on staff knew that I may be more inclined to be trouble, so he checked head to toe! He had me lift my shirt to make sure nothing was hidden. Nope, nothing. He gave me a look that said, "I know you're hiding something, boy!" He even had me lift my cap and tassel to see if there was anything under it! Nothing!

With that, he reluctantly allowed me to enter the gymnasium and take my seat with all the other graduating seniors.

Within a few moments of all us being seated, the audience in the bleachers started to laugh. In the midst of the sea of blue caps, one – namely mine – stood out. You see, I had cut out and attached a Rebel flag to the top of my cap! Shortly thereafter, the coach made his way to my chair, asked me to hand him my cap, and handed me a replacement cap – just blue! I have to admit, that was fun! Once again, I was able to show people that I was a true rebel.

Is hypocrisy something that you struggle with? Do you have any secret sins that you need to confess? It helps to confess your sins to a pastor or another mature Christian, because these people can help keep you from continuing in your bad habits.

Like all the other seniors, I walked on stage to receive my diploma. I shook the principal's hand and took the leather folder that every student received – but it was empty! There was no diploma.

"Victor," the principal said, "you aren't graduating."

What have I done? I thought. I knew my grades had gone down in the second semester, but enough to fail? I wasn't prepared for this.

The next day the assistant principal called me into his office. "Victor," he said, "you didn't have enough credits to graduate, but I'm going to give you a certificate anyway. Do you know why I'm going to let you graduate?"

I shook my head.

"Two reasons. One because I like you, and two because I want you to get out of here and not come back again."

That was fine with me because I planned on leaving town anyway.

chapter sixteen

AN ACAPULCO GETAWAY

My graduation gift from high school was a trip to Acapulco. This made me feel more like an honor student than a person who barely graduated from high school. And guess who was waiting for me in Acapulco? Mr. K., the stepfather from whom we escaped when I was ten years old. He had a beachfront condo and was selling timeshares. My one-week visit was soon extended to three months. Yes, it was a weird situation, but my eyes were blinded with darkness and the lure of drugs, parties, and girls. Obviously, he felt the same way since he extended his hospitality to me.

"I have a job for you," he said. "Are you interested?"

The job involved meeting tourists and encouraging them to listen to a sales presentation about timeshares. I accepted the offer, working by day and partying by night. I even had my own maid to clean up after me. Living at the beachfront condo was the best life I could imagine! One evening I went to a show where the lead performer was a beautiful eighteen-year-old named Lola. After the show I told one of my Mexican friends, "I want to meet her." Laughing he said, "You'll never meet her. She's a star."

What I lacked in common sense I made up for with dogged determination. The security people wouldn't let me near her. So, one night I waited behind the theater for her to exit. When Lola came outside I approached her. She couldn't speak English and my Spanish was bad, but somehow, she understood my invitation to dinner. To my great surprise she accepted so we went out to dinner a few days later. Then we saw each other almost every night after her show. This went on for weeks and Lola even brought me home to meet her parents. After I met her parents I realized she was falling in love. At that point when I knew I couldn't reciprocate her love, I didn't want to mislead her by further seeing her, so I stopped the relationship.

One night I was at a party with about twenty of Mr. K.'s friends. I sat at a table that had a pile of marijuana on it. Somebody took a newspaper and rolled a joint that was two feet long and nearly six inches around. Somebody lit it and we all took hits as it was passed around the table. Then everyone began drinking tequila and I got wasted. Somebody suggested that we go down to the red-light district where there were strip bars, prostitution, and plenty of drugs. So, we went to a nightclub and drank even more tequila. Suddenly I noticed that it was three o'clock in the morning, so I asked the bouncer to call a taxi for me.

"No taxis come here this late," he said in broken English. "No more."

"How do I get back?" I asked.

Grinning, he said, "You'll never make it back."

This is not good, I thought as I started walking down a scary dirt road with my drunken buddy. I had enough street experience to know that I was way out of my element and in grave danger.

We passed a little cantina and stopped in, as if we weren't in a bad enough way. But this ended up providing me something that I'd need in a bit...a weapon in the form of a bottle.

After leaving the cantina and walking a ways, I had to stop because my buddy was wasted, and on the ground in a drunken stupor. Then what my instincts told me might happen, did.

Approaching was a gang of not-so-friendly looking guys. My friend was wasted on the ground beside me in a stupor. He was gonna be of no help to me. I had that bottle in my hand, so I smashed it to have a weapon. In not having much time to think, and no one to help me, I did the only thing I could think of to defend myself in this situation: act like a crazy maniac! I started yelling and screaming, and flailing the broken bottle around in the air. They must've ended up thinking that a nut like me surely wouldn't have anything to steal and they ended up walking away and leaving me be!

We walked all the way to the beach before passing out. The next morning, I awoke under a cabana, knowing I could have been murdered the night before. Once again, I had done something utterly foolish and I should have suffered the consequences of my actions. And once again God had intervened to protect me from myself.

I'm still amazed at how gracious God is. He never says, "I'm fed up with you, stupid!" He will never, never give up on you, so please don't give up on Him! He's patiently waiting to give you a better life than you can ever imagine. Have you surrendered your life to Jesus? If not, what are you waiting for?!

"God has said, 'I will never leave you; I will never abandon you.' Let us be bold then and say, 'The Lord is my helper, I will not be afraid. What can anyone do to me?'" – Hebrews 13:6

"This is good and pleases God our Savior. He wants all people to be saved and to learn the truth." – 1 Timothy 2:3-4

---

chapter seventeen

SEMPER FI, HERE I COME

If you ever saw a poster of bold arrogance, blatant stupidity, and dumb luck, that picture would look like me. When it was time to leave Acapulco after three months, I said goodbye to Lola and my Mexican friends. Then I rolled some marijuana in aluminum foil, wrapped it with coffee grounds, and packed it in my luggage. I could have been locked up in prison forever for trafficking drugs, but instead I didn't get caught. Like I said, dumb luck.

I ended up in Corpus Christi where I got two jobs: I was a bouncer in a country bar by night and a sales clerk in a men's clothing store by day. Then one day the clothing store manager called me into his office.

"Here's the story, Victor," he said. "We know you've been stealing from us. We got you on video."

I tried to lie my way out of it, but he had a pretty good case.

When the truth came out, I had to confess that half of what I was wearing had been stolen from him.

"Now sign this statement of confession. If you don't, you're going to jail."

I got tender and emotional. "Mister, I've had a hard life. I've made some bad choices." I always knew the drama classes would pay off. Then I played my trump card. "You wouldn't throw me in jail when I'm going to serve in the United States Marine Corps."

"Is that the truth, son?"

"Yes sir. I'm going to fight for my country."

The store manager gave it some thought. "If you can prove to me that you're not lying, then I won't have you arrested. But I'm keeping the videotapes of you stealing just in case."

It's a funny thing how I can open my mouth so wide and still get my foot jammed so tight in it. There wasn't much left for me to do except to strip off the stolen contraband and go down to the recruiter's office to keep my promise.

"Golly, Gomer. Here I come!"

chapter eighteen

PREACHER OF THE PLATOON

I felt like a limp balloon caught in a jet stream. My wasted life was out of control and I was now being blown to who-knows-where by the winds of my stupidity and self-destructive behavior. Thankfully the Marine Corps began to give me a sense of direction and purpose. I decided that if I could make it in the Marines, I could make it anywhere. I was hopeful that I could not only survive, but come through with a greater sense of value and purpose.

My boot camp was in San Diego and a Gunnery Sergeant was my Senior Drill Instructor. He was a hardened combat veteran who had served in Vietnam. As soon as I stepped off the bus, we were ordered to stand in yellow footprints painted on the pavement. We had to look straight ahead as the Gunny shouted, "I'm your mother. I'm your father. I'm your worst nightmare!" This guy was psycho. He called me "Thing," saying I wasn't worthy to have a name. He went out of his way to make my life a living hell, probably because I refused to show any signs of intimidation. Some recruits couldn't take the constant brutality and harassment, so they'd slit their wrists to get out. We called them "slashers." Other guys would jump out of second story windows in order to break their legs. The drill instructors didn't seem to care. They only wanted to weed out the wimps.

I might have thought I was scoring a few good points with God by doing my religious duty. But is that what God wants? What does He require of us? How do we please Him? Simply stated, He wants us to cherish Him and His Words (the Bible) more than anything that the world has to offer. How do we do that? We proclaim with our mouth that He is our God, and we prove our love for Him by seeking to obey Him. He also asks us to make a public proclamation of our faith by being baptized.

No, you do not "earn your way to heaven" by your good works. Nobody is good enough. Salvation is a free gift from God! We begin by accepting God's free gift of salvation, and then our good works follow as an expression of love and thanksgiving to God.

One day, Gunny gathered us recruits together. "We need a religious lay leader," he spat. "Who wants to be it?" Nobody moved. We had already learned the painful price of volunteering for anything.

Another drill instructor interjected. "Did any of you go to a Christian or private school?"

I reluctantly raised my hand. "I went to a Christian school for a couple years, Sir."

"Guess what?" Gunny Kern snarled. "You're the new preacher of our platoon!"

I began to feel like a modern-day Jonah. Jonah was a prophet in the Bible who only barely survived being swallowed by a large fish. In a similar way the Marine Corps had devoured every aspect of my life and freedom, and I was now living in the "belly of the beast."

It was my assigned duty to pray for the platoon and offer words of encouragement at the end of each workday. I would always write out my words in advance, making the whole thing rhyme. I'd even toss in some curse words just to spice things up. Clever, I thought. Then at the end of each talk the recruits would say in unison, "Amen!" It was all very straight and regimented like everything else in boot camp. Still I had the feeling that even in the Marines ... God wasn't about to leave me alone.

This is not about looking religious and earning enough points to get on God's good side. It is about having a faithful relationship with a God who loves you so much that He sent His Son Jesus to die on the cross to pay the penalty that you and I deserve.

Have you accepted His free gift of salvation? It's as simple as saying, "Yes God. I surrender my life completely into your hands. I choose to love and obey you more than anything. Forgive my sins and give me a new start. Thank you, Father. You are my only God."

"If you declare that Jesus is Lord and believe that God brought Him back to life, you will be saved." – Romans 10:9

"God saved you through faith as an act of kindness. You had nothing to do with it. Being saved is a gift from God. It's not the result of anything you've done, so no one can brag about it."– Ephesians 2:8-9

"This is His commandment: to believe in His Son, the one named Jesus Christ, and to love each other as He commanded us." – 1 John 3:23

"If you love me, you will obey my commandments." –John 14:15

"Jesus answered him, 'Those who love me will do what I say. My Father will love them, and we will go to them and make our home with them.'" – John 14:23

If you just prayed that prayer to surrender your life to God and serve Him, then let us know! You can contact us at the address in the back of the book. We would love to celebrate this important day with you and pray for you. Let us know if you need a Bible – we'll be happy to send you one. You'll need to grow in your faith, so start going to church and Bible study right away. Let people know about the decision you've made. This is your first step into an incredible destiny! You are a child of God. Welcome to the family!

chapter nineteen

You're Not Leaving Me Behind

I got pneumonia twice while I was in boot camp, but I refused to rest and recuperate. My fellow recruits told me, "You got to go to sick bay."

"No way," I said. "I'll get dropped from the platoon and have to start boot camp all over again. I can't do this twice."

Then when we were leaving for a three-day training hike into the mountains I developed a burning fever. I fought it off as long as I could but finally I started hallucinating. That's when I went to Gunny Kern.

"Sir, I request permission to go to sick bay, Sir!"

"Are you dying?" Gunny Kern asked.

"Sir, no, Sir."

"Request denied." Gunny smiled.

I held on for two more days until we started back down the mountain. I was staggering and stumbling, barely able to put one foot in front of the other. The two junior drill instructors caught me as I passed out. They called an ambulance and rushed me to the naval hospital on base. By the time I got to the emergency room my temperature was 104 degrees. A Navy doctor put an IV in me and sent me to the San Diego Naval Hospital for further treatment. The Navy doctors in San Diego found that I was dehydrated; my lungs were filled with fluid and I had pneumonia. One of the doctors said to me, "Son, you almost died. If you want I can get you out of the Marine Corps right now. All you have to do is sign this piece of paper." I sat up in my bed as tears filled my eyes. "You don't know what I been through to get here. I ain't got nothin' to go back to if I don't make it in the Marines." I refused to sign the paper.

The doctor reported the negligence of Gunny to the company commander and he was disciplined. I was put on light duty for the rest of my time in boot camp. I was so proud to walk off the parade field after the graduation ceremony. I was a United States Marine. Nobody could take that away from me. My only disappointment was that no one from my family was able to come to share my greatest sense of accomplishment.

The two junior drill instructors shook my hand and one of them said, "I never thought you'd make it after all you went through."

"I'm proud to call you my fellow Marine," the other added. "Any time I can help you, let me know."

The Gunnery Sergeant cursed me. I had accomplished what I set out to do and not even he could diminish my sense of self-worth. I had done it! And considering where I had been just thirteen weeks earlier, this was not a bad place to be in my life.

chapter twenty

MOJAVE AND MARTIAL ARTS

After boot camp, the Marine Corps assigned me to Radio Operator School at their Twenty-Nine Palms base in the Mojave Desert. It wasn't as tough as boot camp but a whole lot hotter. On my 19th birthday – July 5, 1984 – the temperature was 127 degrees. I graduated from Radio Operator School near the top of the class and was recommended to High Frequency Communications School. My radio and television experience helped me tie for first place student in the class.

There was a church near the base that I started attending with some of my fellow Marines. My heart wasn't really into it, but I went anyway. It was at this time that I also got involved in martial arts. The Marine Corps offered a self-defense program to active duty Marines and I was an eager participant. I weighed 155 pounds and would fight or spar with anyone. I didn't care about winning. I just wanted to learn new techniques. At first, I wasn't much good and these guys who weighed 200 pounds or more would knock me down flat. But I'd get right back up and say, "Not bad." I got in my share of licks though because I was a scrappy dude, kinda like trying to hold a little cat in a sink of water! You might do it for a little while, but it won't be fun!

When my training in the Mojave Desert was completed, I was assigned to permanent duty at Camp Pendleton, California. That's when I was able to attend the highly reputable IMB Academy for martial arts in Torrance. This school was famous because its instructor, Dan Inosanto, had been one of Bruce Lee's top students. I trained hard and learned various fighting styles: Kenpo from Ron Jimenez, kickboxing from Joe Lewis and Bill Wallace, and Brazilian Jiu-Jitsu from the Gracie Family. Remember how I had practiced playing the trumpet for five hours a day when I was a boy? Well, I did the same with martial arts. I would work out early in the morning and again when I got off work. It's crazy how passionate I was about fighting. It was becoming a part of me … too big of a part.

Oceanside, California, was a rough town at that time. After Vietnam, there were a lot of former Marines with combat post-traumatic stress disorder who were always looking for a fight in Oceanside. There were also a lot of gangs who liked to prey on young and inexperienced Marines. Three gang members confronted me and a friend while we were on liberty in Oceanside.

"Give us your money!" they demanded.

"We ain't giving you any money," I said matter-of-factly. Then thinking quickly, I added, "Do you know who you're talking to? We're undercover military police officers and we're on a stakeout. We've got two cars following us, and I expect you boys better be moving."

The gang backed off. Suddenly my fellow Marine took off running – or as they say, he "attacked to the rear."

"You're lying to us," the biggest gang member said as he boldly stepped forward.

One of them ripped a gold chain from around my neck. Then the biggest guy found a letter to my momma that contained some money. I grabbed the letter.

"Not that," I said. "It's a letter to my mom."

The big guy pulled back his fist to hit me and I saw that his ring had a pointed object on it. Instantly I grabbed his head and stuck my thumb into his eye. The man screamed. I then turned my attention to the other two men and began punching them.

Pop, pop, pop! Smack! Crack! Kinda like an old Batman movie.

Ultimately it was the big guy who grabbed me from behind, picked me off my feet, and threw me to the ground. The three men kept kicking me until I stopped moving. It's a good old Southern trick: when you're outnumbered, play 'possum like you're dead.

"Man, we killed him!" one of them yelled. "Let's get out of here!"

They turned and ran. I waited a minute before rising. My clothes were bloody and torn. I found my fellow Marine at a gas station. He explained that he had gone to look for a weapon, although I wondered why he hadn't helped me with the five-fingered weapons at the end of his arms. Another Marine was at the gas station, so I asked him for a weapon. He went to his car and brought back a big knife. I took it and went looking for the gang who beat me up, but I couldn't find them.

On many paydays for several months afterwards I walked the same alley looking for that gang, hoping to get revenge. I thank God that I never found them because if I did who knows what would have happened – nothing good for them, and even worse for me I'm sure.

Does revenge ever pay off? I don't think so. You take revenge, then the other guy (or the other guy's family) takes revenge on you, you take revenge again, and it keeps escalating. It's like the Mafia, or gangs in L.A., or the Arabs and Israelis. These guys have been carrying grudges for so many generations that they probably don't even remember what caused the fighting in the first place.

Jesus had a new idea that is totally mind- boggling. He said that we should give love to people who hate us, and bless people who curse us. It sounds crazy, but it's the only way to end the fighting. And here's what I've learned first-hand – when you give love and bless the guy who hurts you, that feels a thousand times better than hurting him back. You ought to try it sometime!

"Love your enemies, do good to those who hate you, bless those who curse you, and pray for those who mistreat you. If anyone hits you on one cheek, let him hit the other one too; if someone takes your coat, let him have your shirt as well. Give to everyone who asks you for something, and when someone takes what is yours, do not ask for it back. Do for others just what you want them to do for you. If you love only the people who love you, why should you receive a blessing? Even sinners love those who love them! ... No! Love your enemies and do good to them; lend and expect nothing back. You

will then have a great reward, and you will be children of the Most High God. For he is good to the ungrateful and the wicked." – Luke 6:27-35 (GNB)

So, I have learned my best weapon is forgiveness. It's more powerful than you can imagine. I'm not saying I'm a pacifist because that is not biblical. It's just better to surrender your sinful anger than let it turn to bitterness and control you.

chapter twenty-one

ANOTHER NEAR-DEATH EXPERIENCE

During my time in the Marines I became proficient with a .45 caliber pistol and M16 rifle. I can't explain how cool it was to be issued a real military grade weapon. I thought to myself, "This is awesome! I get to shoot bad people, I won't go to jail, and they will pay me for this!"

I could put ten rounds into a target that was five and a half football fields away with no scope. This ability, plus my desire to teach other Marines, enabled me to graduate at the top of my class at the Primary Marksman Instructor School, and go on to compete as a competitive shooter in the First Marine Division Matches. Then I accepted an invitation to become a weapons instructor. My duty was to train Marines to properly shoot and handle M16A1/A2 service rifles and the .45 caliber pistol. I also began teaching hand-to-hand combat and training in different kinds of martial arts.

I had a lot going for me in the Marines. I had accomplished so much through martial arts, but I couldn't attain the inner peace that should have been my primary goal in the first place. It was as if I was searching for something that was always out of reach ... just around the corner. I didn't even know what I was searching for. I got a punching board and hit it over and over to build up my hands and knuckles for fighting. I would meditate to a point where I could hit the board until the flesh ripped off my hands and still barely experience any pain. I abused my hand so much that I couldn't move it for three weeks. The result of that ongoing punishment still shows on my knuckles to this day.

One day I had a life changing experience that I will never forget. I was sitting on a CH 46 Sea Knight helicopter in full gear with my M16 rifle.

Suddenly a crew chief I'd never seen before ran up and yelled, "Get out! Get out of there!" I motioned, "Me?"

He nodded so I jumped out of the chopper. The man directed me to a second bird that was standing by. The blades were whirring, and dust was blowing everywhere. We lifted off with the other helicopter behind us as we practiced maneuvers. As we crossed a mountain range I noticed that the other chopper was no longer following us, and then we were immediately grounded. That's when we learned that the other helicopter had crashed, killing everyone on board. I couldn't believe it! I had been on that helicopter and God had rescued me! I guess it wasn't my time to die. Once more I couldn't ignore the message.

It was as if God's voice was saying, "I've kept you alive, Victor, because I have something planned for you." I couldn't help but remember the prophecies that had been given to me.

I didn't know the Marine Corps crew chief that had ordered me off the doomed helicopter, and I still don't know why he did it. Neither helicopter was overcrowded. I shed tears that day for the Marines who died in the crash. I almost died with them. A wave of sadness still sweeps over me when I think about those men.

chapter twenty-two

New Beginnings

I enrolled in several accelerated college courses that were funded by the Marine Corps. My grades were good and for a time I even considered becoming a lawyer. One evening my speech professor asked everyone to take out a piece of paper and a pen. "I want you to write down ten things that are most important to you," he said.

I listed my family first, martial arts second and God third. It's easy to make excuses why God is not first in our lives. But none – not one – is valid before our Creator who gave us life. I knew in my conscience that we are not supposed to have any other gods before God Almighty. It started to bother me that God was not in the rightful place in my life. After the assignment I began to think that it was time to straighten out my priorities. I knew that God should be first in my life. So, I made a commitment to stop partying and become more responsible.

I knew that my friend J.J. would be invaluable in helping me accomplish this goal. J.J. was the only true Christian among my closest friends in the Marine Corps. My other friends included a stocky black man from Lake Charles named Carter, and Jesse who was a gang-banger type of guy. The four of us always hung out together. Every Wednesday night J.J. would invite me to church with him. I'd be wearing my best nightclub clothes, and he probably got used to my predictable reply.

"No thanks, J.J. It's Ladies Night at the club. Maybe next time."

"Okay Vic," J.J. would respond. "Have a good time, and be careful."

J.J. could have kept "preaching at me" and telling me how bad I was. But I probably wouldn't have listened. His greatest witness was his consistency, his genuine faith and most importantly – his love. That reminds me of the early Christians who lived just after Jesus went back up into heaven. Love is what set these Christians apart.

"All the believers kept meeting together and they shared everything with each other. From time to time, they sold their property and other possessions and distributed the money to anyone who needed it. The believers had a single purpose and went to the temple every day. They were joyful and humble as they ate at each other's homes and shared their food. At the same time, they praised God and had the good will of all the people. Every day the Lord saved people and they were added to the group." – Acts 2:44-47

"The greatest love you can show is to give your life for your friends." –John 15:13

"We understand what love is when we realize that Christ gave His life for us. That means we must give our lives for other believers." – 1 John 3:16

J.J. was never judgmental. Even if he couldn't agree with my behavior he still loved me with God's love and it showed. Once again someone had seen something loveable in me that I could not. He'd also invite me to church on Sunday mornings. I always gave him the same old answer.

"Maybe next week."

That was the routine. The following week J.J would try again. And the following week he'd get the same answer. One thing I noticed though: J.J. exhibited an amazing consistency and stamina in his commitment to the Lord. He was even more dedicated to God than I was to the martial arts. That made a big impression on me.

Meanwhile I knew that something significant was missing in my life. I had a huge hole not only in my chest but in my heart as well. My soul felt terribly empty. So, I tried to keep myself busy with school, with work, with martial arts, with nightclubs, with physical pursuits, with fun and games. But nothing gave me the satisfaction that I needed. It was like trying to patch a twenty-foot hole in the Goodyear blimp with a tiny rubber patch.

I was impressed at how J.J. embraced the truth of the Bible. On the other hand, I ran from God's truth. J.J. welcomed God's truth as an ally that enabled him to overcome insurmountable obstacles. God's Word was a burning beacon to guide him down life's darkened highway. I watched J.J. practice purity and avoid sin and overcome temptation. As for me, I was living out the words of that old country song, "Lead me not into temptation – I can find my way all by myself."

On New Year's Eve in 1985, my buddy Carter and I drove to Los Angeles where we clubbed all night until we ended up at a bar in South Central. Carter was too wiped out to go inside so he stayed in my car while I walked up to the bouncer at the door. He was a big black guy about the size of Montana.

"Are you lost?" he boomed down on me from on high.

"I ain't lost," I said as I walked inside. I noticed that I was the only white guy in the club, but that didn't matter to me. So, I stepped up to the first pretty girl I saw and asked her to dance. Immediately the music stopped dead and a chilling silence filled the room. All eyes were focused on me and several men began coming in my direction. I might not be the smartest guy around, but I quickly figured out that they were not coming to wish me a happy New Year.

"I'll see you later," I called over my shoulder to my abandoned dance partner. I sprinted out the door and across the street as fast as I possibly could. All the while I'm screaming, "Carter! Carter! Start the car, Carter! Start the car!"

Carter threw open the driver's door for me, and we got out of there!

Actually, something of lasting worth came out of that night. As we drove back to Camp Pendleton I was thinking about what a waste I was making of my life – all the stupid situations I'd put myself into and how many times I should have gotten myself killed. By this time, I was driving, and Carter was sound asleep. So, I turned on the radio.

"New beginnings," a man said. "If any man be in Christ, he is a new creature."

"What?" I said as I took my hand away from the dial.

Pastor Greg Laurie of Harvest Christian Fellowship was speaking about Jesus and new beginnings. As the sun rose over the eastern hills on this new day in a new year, something out of the ordinary had just gotten my attention. I turned up the volume, so I wouldn't miss a word.

"New beginnings."

It was as if a lamp had been switched on in the darkness. Could I be hearing God's voice? At the end of the message, the announcer said, "Tune in tomorrow at this same time."

So, early the next morning I was up and in my freezing car with the radio on. I didn't want anyone to know that I was listening to a preacher on Christian radio. But I began to listen regularly to Pastor Greg Laurie. I also listened to Pastor Chuck Smith, who was Greg Laurie's mentor. I told myself, "For a grandpa-sounding guy, he makes pretty good sense too!"

Pastor Raul Ries' teachings on the radio also impacted me. First, you can't ignore his thick Spanish accent! I thought, "Cool, KWVE brought in a missionary from Mexico to teach the Bible on the radio!" He also has a martial arts background, which drew my interest. But I soon realized that this thickly accented dude was teaching the Bible in an awesome way and came to learn that Pastor Raul was the Senior Pastor at one of the largest churches in California, Calvary Chapel Golden Springs.

Listening to Christian radio soon became the highlight of my day. Good things were beginning to happen. I sensed a new beginning. But there was still one surprise that was about to totally knock my socks off.

The world is filled with voices– voices of friends, parents, teachers, the media, voices in your head, constant voices. All the while God's voice is gently whispering to us – through our conscience and through the things that we know in our heart to be true. It's obvious that I was listening more to the temptations of the world, while J.J. was listening to God's voice. Whose voice are you listening to? Listen – you need to spend time listening to God, so you can hear His voice. And there's no better way to hear God than to read the Bible, or to listen to people who are teaching the Bible. All the voices of the world bring death. But God's voice brings life!

[Jesus said:] "The words that I have spoken to you are spiritual. They are life." – John 6:63

"The words of the Lord are true, and all His works are dependable." – Psalm 33:4

"Your Word is a lamp for my feet and a light for my path." – Psalm 119:105

chapter twenty-three

A Life Changing Letter

I was sitting in my barracks when someone brought me a letter addressed to Vaughn Victor Kennedy Marx. The name "Marx" was written in lower-case letters. In the top left-hand corner of the envelope was the name Karl W. Marx. I stared at the envelope in disbelief. This was a letter from my biological father. I had only seen him a few times in my entire life. It's difficult to describe the mingled emotions of curiosity and fear and pain and desire that were crowding through my brain. What would this "blood" stranger have to say? And why would he write me now? I first saw Karl Marx when I was six years old and our paths crossed several times after that. But the encounters were brief and trivial. My gut feeling was that this man meant nothing to me. I opened the envelope and nearly reacted with disgust when I read the first line.

"Dear Son."

I'm not your son! I thought. "To whom it may concern" would be more appropriate.

I continued reading. He wrote with remorse about his decadent lifestyle. He was sorry about his mistakes and his apology seemed to be so sincere. He had been a wild man and had spent time in a mental hospital. Then my eyes locked onto one sentence:

"I know you're going to think I'm crazy, but I've gone crazy for Jesus Christ." He then claimed to have become born again in Christ. I was speechless! This couldn't be the same incorrigible old man who was hopelessly beyond redemption. At times I thought an empty beer can was worth more than the Karl that I knew. I didn't even know the word "God" was in his vocabulary, except maybe in a string of dirty expletives.

Then Karl invited me to come and visit him. The invitation intrigued me. Plain logic and a ten second review of this man's history would have caused me to squash that invitation, throw it in the rubbish, and never give another thought about this man. Instead I held that piece of paper tight while my thoughts wandered. What if the things he said were true? I remembered that my thirty-day leave was coming up. I took another glance at the handwritten words on that page. Suddenly my mind was made up. I was going to visit my father.

There was a stronger force than logic at work here. I believe I was beginning to hear God's voice. This burning desire to see my father was strangely connected to the spiritual fire that was slowly growing in my heart. I was beginning to heed the call that God had placed on my life, to know Him and make Him known. I knew there would have to be some more changes in my life and I believed that God would make His plan clear to me in time. For now, I needed to see Karl Marx. And I needed to wait for God's plan to be revealed.

Then a wrench was thrown into my plans. I had carelessly stored some contraband martial arts weapons in my locker. That's when I received a surprise visit from a Marine officer.

"Don't touch anything," he ordered as we stood at attention by our racks. "This is a search for contraband and drugs."

He eyed my trophies. "I know you're a martial arts guy. Do you have any weapons here?"

"No, sir, I don't," I replied, looking him straight in the eye.

He smiled. "Really? I got a report you've got weapons here."

The officer then opened my wall locker and took a quick glance. My weapons were concealed behind some books and he didn't see them.

"All right," he said. Then he left.

I sighed in relief, but it was only a momentary reprieve. Unexpectedly the Marine officer returned. He walked straight to my wall locker, moved a couple of books, and felt around for weapons. My sharpened kama – a martial arts weapon – cut his hand.

"No weapons, huh?"

I had to stand before a panel of Marine officers. My charges were lying to an officer and possessing illegal contraband. I told the panel of officers that I was scheduled to see my biological father on a thirty-day leave.

At one time I thought nothing of lying, cheating, hurting people, breaking the law, or even hurting myself. I didn't care what the law had to say because I was "a law unto myself." (Romans 2:14) That's scary and dangerous, when a person gets so deceived that he thinks right is wrong and wrong is right. Watch out! Satan is so sly and seductive that he can make his poison taste like candy. You seriously believe that wrong is right. But it will kill you in the end.

"There is a way that seems right to a person, but eventually it ends in death." – Proverbs 14:12

"Even Satan can disguise himself to look like an angel of light." – 2 Corinthians 11:14 (GNB)

"Make no mistake about this: You can never make a fool out of God. Whatever you plant is what you'll harvest. If you plant in the soil of your corrupt nature, you will harvest destruction. But if you plant in the soil of your spiritual nature, you will harvest everlasting life." – Galatians 6:7-8

"It's cancelled. You're under house arrest. You are confined to your quarters."

The book had been thrown in my face and rightly so because I deserved it. In defeat I asked once more to be allowed to go on leave and for some reason this time they decided to let me go. A Marine captain who practiced martial arts intervened on my behalf. I would have to face the court when I returned, and I would certainly receive strict discipline. Then they warned me not to go "AWOL" before they had a chance to finish their business with me. I assured the court that I would be back and that I'd willingly face any punishment that they thought was appropriate.

Once more I had screwed up and once more someone had rescued me.

While I was on the plane to Louisiana, I had a ton of mixed emotions about meeting my father. When I arrived in Baton Rouge, Karl was there to meet me. He was fifty years old, but he looked seventy. His hard living had taken a merciless toll on him. His nose was flattened by too many fights and his skin was leathery and wrinkled. But I saw an aura of inner peace that had never been there before. As you can imagine, this visit with my biological father was extremely memorable.

Still I was totally unprepared for the profound impact he was about to have on my life. You couldn't dam the Mississippi River and make a bigger impact on me than this.

TWAIN MARK LOOKING FOR TROUBLE
This lightweight of the George Oden stable has fought only 20 professional bouts but has won 16 of them. Mark is a crowd-pleaser who has never failed to put up a good bout on the Coast.

My grandfather, Twain Marx: Prize Fighter and Professional Boxer; fought at Madison Square Garden

Victor Jay Boutte –
Victor's Namesake

Karl Marx –
Victor's Father

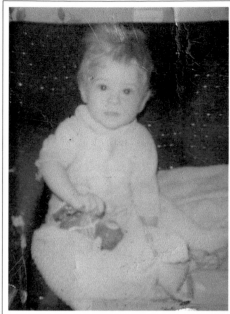

Victor as a baby and toddler

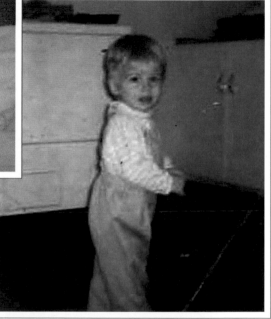

Little Victor with his
funnel chest

Victor with his rifle

Home on Bayou in Louisiana with the alligators

My martial arts career allowed me to use it as a
platform to share my faith.

Marines 1986

Victor as a weapons
instructor

Me and my attitude

Catching air with a flying side-kick!

Always time for humor!

I was seriously intense...intensley serious!

Me as a young hard-charging Marine

Loved kicking! (That's my little Cutlass Supreme the Lord told me to leave at the alter...sold it for $1 to fellow Marine to keep transporting Marines to church...)

Doing a flying sidekick over kid's back to break board held by not so willing holders

Early days with Cho Hee II - a prominent Koren-American master of Taekwondo, holding the rank of 9th dan in the martial art (notice our calloused knuckles.)

Me and Joe Lewis July 1985 at a seminar in Vista, California

My Dad, Karl
Mark, aka Le Tigre,
bouncer and feared
street fighter

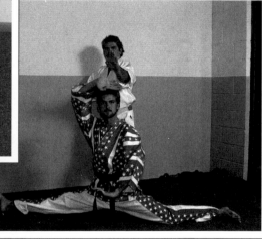

With my Dad, Founder
of Keichu-Do

Dad throwing me at my first dojo

With my dad goofing around
practicing Hollywood stunts

My competitive nature pays off

My martial arts career allowed me to use it as a platform to share my faith.

Amazing restoration between father and son

My razor-sharp samurai sword

Victor cutting a watermelon on his student with Nathan Bardeen and Bismark watching

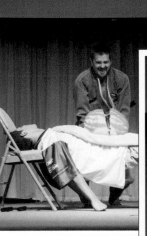

Start of the downcut with razor sharp-sword

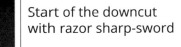

Fully in the moment. Notice blade at very bottom.

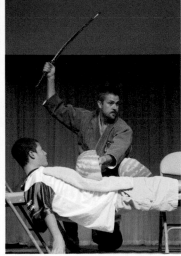

Family friend, Josh Loo says, "Thank you, Jesus, it worked!

Photos by Bob Simon

107

Eileen became my bride in 1988

Papa Marx and Victor with little Shiloh at his first tournament

Karate Star Magazine Cover

All my kids have been brought up in the dojo

Three generations (my boy is a full grown man now)

Fumio Demura
Legendary Karate Master

Carlos Machado JiuJitsu and Chuck Norris' Instructor

The hold I used to subdue the attempted rapist in Hawaii

Blessed living in Hawaii – Running Martial Arts School in Waikiki

Bas Ruttan

Jiu-Jitsu legend,
Professor Wally Jay

With 5X UFC Champion,
Frank Shamrock

Amazing location near Victor and Eileen's home in Hawaii.

Sharing a message of true freedom through Christ at a July 4th Freedom Celebration in Garden Grove, CA

Pastor Chuck Smith and Brian Broderson: Victor's pastors in California

God restores what "the locusts steal" (Joel 2:25) Never too late to be a dad!

Dad and his life-changing letter to me

"What's amazing is that Victor survived his childhood and what is even more amazing is that the Lord is using him now to reach so many hurting youth." Dr. James Dobson

The Marxes and the Dobsons

Pastor Chuck praying for me and ATP Ministries. I can't stress how important it is for every believer to find great Bible teaching an other mature believers whose spiritual walk you can model.

Hanging out with music artists, The Katinas, after a Harvest Crusade!

With musician Toby Mac

With my Eileen and musical artist, Chris Tomlin

With legendary NFL Quarterback, Brett Favre.

Greg Laurie

Sword Demo at Gainesville State School

Gainesville State School screening The Victor Marx Story

Don Antonio Lugo High School Assembly–Sword Demo

"If we help build a kid now, we won't have
to repair an adult later."

Victor praying with a
BlackMat MMA student

This is my passion-to join Jesus in setting young captives free!

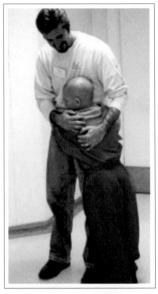

"I was in prison and you visited Me."-Matthew 25:36

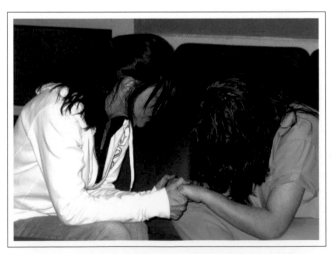

Eileen praying with an incareted teen girl, a precious child of God

Chael Sonnen, UFC Fighter

Victor at Teen Challenge Flordia: Kids
and Dads accepted Jesus as Savior...
Glory to God!

Victor at Boys Republic, Chino, California

Victor in a strangle hold by
legendary Martial Artist, Wrestler,
and Actor - Gene LeBell

Victor with Dave Loyst, Gene LeBell, Gokor
Chivchyan, Jim Wooley and Jim West

My razor-sharp samurai sword

Victor Marx:
Tough not Hard

Meekness – power under control!

I used to think I needed to be 'hard' because of all the violence in my life. But a hard heart cannot give or receive love. With God's grace I learned how to be 'tough.'

As a tough guy, I can deal with my past and live my greatest dreams.

—Victor Marx

God has abundantly blessed me with five children!
"Blessed is the man whose quiver is full of them."
-Psalms 127:5

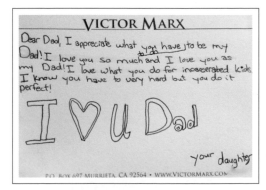

Sweet note from my little
daughter... she gets it! And
encourages her dad

Letters from lockedup youth:
"I answer back all kids who
write me." - Victor

My brother in the Lord, NFL Linebacker, Kevin Burnett with me at my ATP Keichu-Do Training Academy

Eileen and I honored to meet President George W. Bush at his annual Warrior Open benefiting wounded warriors

With Soul Surfer, Bethany Hamilton

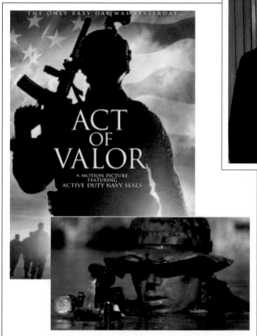

Navy SEAL Senior Chief
Dave Hansen in movie,
Act of Valor

With Senior Chief Dave Hansen
Navy Seal in Act of Valor

Life Today T.V. Interview with
James and Betty Robison - 2012

With Actor Bob Saget

With Actor Mathew Perry

With our friend and brother, Nick Vujicic

Mike, Victor's brother displaying his recently killed alligators

The actual pecan tree where they hung the molester to scare him

Commercial Cooler site (Chicken houses in the background)

Mammaw's porch where my family wrapped me up to thaw out after they rescued me from the cooler

Back on the Bayou where I lived

With Ms. Lillie Barron (in the house she bought from Mr. K. and from which we escaped) and Ms. Betty Carlisle to whose home we escaped for refuge with our Maw Maw.

Victor and Eileen Marx at the April 26, 2012 World Film Premiere of The Victor Marx Story: When Impossible is The Only Way Out!

With my bride Eileen
24 years later

The Heart of Marriage is
love as God intended it to
be. (1st Corinthians 13:4-8)

Still wielding the
"Sword of the Spirit,
which is the Word of
God" (Ephesians 6:17)

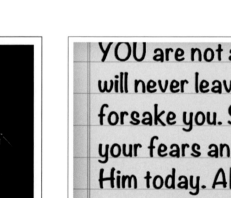

YOU are not alone, Jesus will never leave you or forsake you. Surrender your fears and anxieties to Him today. Abide in His peace. Forsake wrong choices and embrace His way of right living, His love is more powerful than your bitterness. - victor marx

Bobby Little–Executive Director Christian Embassy
Washington DC

Col. Jason T. Garkey Regimental Commander 3D US
Infantry Presenting Victor with a Plaque for speaking to
the Old Guard.

2017 Iraq

After our 6th trip into the region, we decided to obtain long term residence cards and a home. Many doors of opportunity opened to help so many hurting people.

Victor with FTO as they are in Iraq helping those just getting liberated from ISIS

Victor meeting with a very influential Muslim leader in the Middle East. Sheikh Abdlatif Al-Humayim. The Sheikh was shot by an ISIS fighter 24 hours after this meeting.

General Mustafa and his wife with Victor and Eileen. The General was showing us his home town.

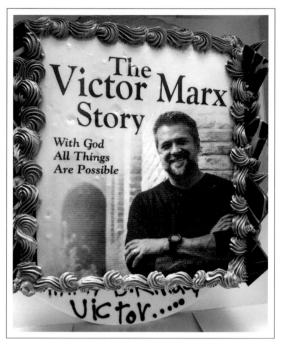

General Mustafa and his family made this birthday cake
using the photo of Victor's book in Iraq.

Enjoying dinner in special Birthday outfit

Victor on special training operation with the elite UH60 Blackhawk crew-doing infill and exfill training, and getting great footage for the film.

Victor with the Free Burma Rangers, working on the wounded on the front lines in Iraq, and providing food and water for those fleeing from ISIS in Mosul.

Victor with Scout. A mortar had just exploded and hit 30 yards from where Victor was sitting. Either our days are numbered or they are not.

Baby Ali with Scout

Where evil is manifest in people like ISIS I believe
in protective angels and carrying grenades.

Victor with Dave Eubank

FTO Team helping Shia Militia fighters after a VBED car bomb
exploded on us in a village outside of Mosul.

Ret. Lt. Col. Oliver North USMC with Victor in Iraq

Iraqis love taking pictures even during missions.

Snapshot of little girls reading the comic book of Victor's
story in Arabic

Victor met this young man at one of the IDP camps in Iraq. He is the only one left in his family after ISIS killed all of his family. Victor prayed for him and his future, that he would be the young man God created him to be.

Precious little girl just liberated out of Mosul

Boys in the camps waiting to get a Lion and Lamb

This young man gave us a middle finger salute as our vehicle drove through the camp.

There are a number of ISIS families living in these IDP camps. Grateful to provide their children with Lions and Lambs.

This young woman was recently freed from being held by ISIS. Her biggest fear was not ever being able to get married. Great news, about 1 year after this photo was taken she did get engaged, married and moved to a safe country.

General Mustafa, 9th Armored Division of the Iraqi Army holding baby Ali.

Baby Ali with General Mustafa. He was rescued by the Iraqi Army after his parents were killed by ISIS machine gunners.

General Mustafa cares for all people and showed great compassion in freeing thousands from ISIS.

Baby Ali captured all of our hearts

During heavy fighting this little girl was found and pulled from the rubble after after her parents died because of ISIS. General Mustafa called Victor and asked us to do a recovery mission for this little girl whose life they saved.

We named this little precious girl "Boo"

Her older sister was found a few days after we had her and they were reunited! However, both girls are now orphans.

This is the little girl who had been found in the rubble just days after we received her.

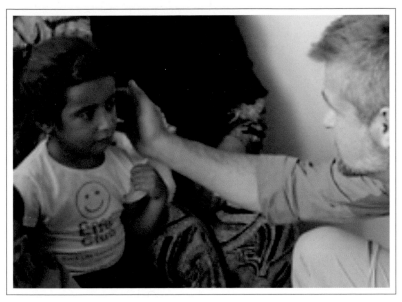

This little one was found hiding under her mother's dress for
two or three days after her mother was shot dead by ISIS,
only coming out to look for water among the dead bodies.

Her name is Damaeah. In Arabic, her name
means "tear."

My daughter and Damaeah, this little one came out of her distraught state and was laughing and learning how to blow bubbles.

Victor and Damaeah laughing and enjoying a moment of escape.

Victor with the families liberated from ISIS, handing out Lions and Lambs.

Mohammed on later mission was shot 8x by ISIS and lived! When he was in the hospital in Baghdad this multi-generational Muslim told the team, "Don't worry, Jesus is in my heart now!"

Victor & Shaheen, his "adopted" son, who also worked closely with Yazidis at ATP and FBR. Sadly this champion of children was killed by an ISIS sniper while part of a rescue team helping a wounded girl and her father.

Uncle Si of Duck Dynasty

Victor speaking at men's event in Virginia with Uncle Si also being one of the speakers.

This photo shoot was for the DVD cover of *Triggered Too*

Filming Triggered!

Behind the scenes of our Triggered Film

Triggered Military & Triggered Too

Now available on DVD at
victormarx.com

chapter twenty-four

FINDING TWO FATHERS AND A HOME

One Sunday evening Karl invited me to go to a service at the church he was attending.

"You'll like it," he said. "A lot of Black Belts go there with me."

Even though I had always called myself a Christian, I knew I had been backsliding and running away from my faith since I was six years old. I would take two steps forward and one step back. Or sometimes three steps back. I acted like a Christian when it was easy or when it didn't interfere with my personal pleasures and vices. It was fake Christianity on my terms, not on God's.

Well, I did go that night, and something strange happened in that church. I thought of Jesus dying just for me, and for the first time in my life I was truly sorry for my sins. Silently I began to weep. I wondered how mad God must be at me for the mess I'd made of my life. But as I sat there I heard the Lord's voice – not audibly, but quietly inside me. He was saying, "I love you. I love you. I love you."

What's that all about? How could the Lord possibly love me after all that I've done to Him? My life has been one failure after another. I've done nothing to earn anybody's love.

Still those words continued. "I love you. I love you. I love you." Suddenly I became emotional. And I didn't like it. Tears were splashing on the pages of my borrowed Bible, causing them to wrinkle.

"Stop crying!" I told myself. "This is embarrassing. Don't cry. You're a Marine! You got a tattoo for goodness' sake!" But nothing could shut off my tears. The pastor invited people to come forward for prayer, saying, "If you need to get things right with God, you can do that tonight."

I couldn't resist any longer. With tears flowing I moved out of my pew, knocking over an old grey-haired woman in the process.

"I'm sorry," I said.

"Honey," she said with a smile, "it's okay. Just get down there."

I actually ran forward and fell at the altar. My embarrassment was gone, and I didn't care what anyone thought of me anymore. Hundreds of people were in that church, but that moment it was only God and me. I had a huge load of junk to dump at His feet – all those years of rage and hate and filth and shame spilled out – a gigantic, ugly monolith of sin came forth from the blackness of my heart. And then the most incredible thing happened. Miraculously it all disappeared like a wisp of smoke.

It just disappeared. I knew I was forgiven.

A man's hand rested gently on my shoulder. "Brother, can I pray for you?"

I spun around with a cocked fist. "Don't you ever touch me again or I'll break your jaw," I snarled. "This is between me and God."

My dad, who at that point had come down front because he saw me racing to the altar, was sitting on the pew, and had his arms stretched open wide across the back of it, said matter-of-factly to the man, "Hey, I know the boy...he'll hit you so leave him be."

"Sorry," the man said as he backed away.

I continued to cry out to God, "I don't have much to give, but whatever I have is yours. All of it. If you can use me, then you can have me."

I almost heard God laugh. He immediately reminded me of those two prophecies that had been given me so many years before. And what a joy it was to finally walk into my heavenly Father's destiny. I continued to kneel and bask in His presence for a good long time. My heart was clean and forgiven. I felt like a newborn baby.

When I finally got up to go, my dad was the only one sitting in the pews. And he had the biggest smile smeared across his face. He didn't say anything, but he knew that God had gotten a hold of me. I went back to his apartment feeling as if the weight of the whole world had been lifted off my shoulders.

Later I told him about my little problem at Camp Pendleton and about the uncertain future that awaited me. His advice was simple and straightforward.

"Just tell them the truth, son."

It was a great piece of advice. Why didn't I think of that? I'd already been rehearsing some good lies for when I returned.

Then as I left Baton Rouge I suddenly realized – I don't even know how it happened but – the man I called Karl Marx had somehow become my Dad. And God was looking like a Father to me as well.

In one day I had found two fathers and one eternal home.

Have you heard the story of the Prodigal Son in the Bible? Jesus told that story. It's about a boy who took his family inheritance (before his father was even dead yet!) and he left home. He partied until he was so poor that he had to rob the pigs for something to eat. That's when he came to his senses and decided to go back home and tell his father that he was sorry. I love the way this father treated him when he returned. It's really a picture of God – our perfect Father is waiting patiently for each one of us to come home.

Here's how the story ends:

"So, he went at once to his father. While he was still at a distance, his father saw him and felt sorry for him. He ran to his son, put his arms around him, and kissed him. Then his son said to him, 'Father, I've sinned against heaven and you. I don't deserve to be called your son anymore.' The father said to his servants, 'Hurry! Bring out the best robe and put it on him. Put a ring on his finger and sandals on his

feet. Bring the fattened calf, kill it, and let's celebrate with a feast. My son was dead and has come back to life. He was lost but has been found.' Then they began to celebrate." – Luke 15:20-24 chapter twenty-five

TO TELL THE TRUTH

I kept my word. I said I would return to face the panel of judges and that's exactly what I did. The charges of lying to an officer and possessing contraband were read aloud. I was then asked if I was going to plead innocent or guilty.

"Guilty," I said without hesitation.

Everyone's mouth seemed to drop open simultaneously. This was clearly not what they had expected. They knew me to be wild and rebellious – "Thumper" was my nickname because of my violent temper. They'd say, "Don't mess with Victor or he's gonna thump you." And they knew I would! The lieutenant, in particular, looked thrilled about my plea. As for me, I felt great. The truth is empowering. I wasn't shackled with trying to remember any well-rehearsed lies.

"But may I give an explanation?" I asked the court.

"Speak."

So, I continued. "I just want to say that when I got busted, I planned on coming back here and lying about it. In fact, I made up some pretty good lies. But something happened to me when I was on leave. I went to church with my dad and God got a hold of my life. I now want to tell you the truth. I lied to the officer. I hid those weapons. I was wrong but I'm telling you now that I'm changed. I'm not gonna lie no more. Would y'all please forgive me? Whatever you want to give me for a sentence, I deserve it and I will take it. I'm able to tell the truth because God has come into my life in a real and amazing way."

> *Like my daddy said, it's always better to tell the truth. You don't want to tell your best friend a big lie, then you tell your sister a different version of the story, and they get to comparing notes. Bad news! Has that ever happened to you? It's way better to just tell the truth. That's what God thinks too.*
>
> *"Never steal, lie, or deceive your neighbor." – Leviticus 19:11*
>
> *"Lips that lie are disgusting to the Lord, but honest people are His delight." – Proverbs 12:22*
>
> *"The devil was a murderer from the beginning. He has never been truthful. He doesn't know what the truth is. Whenever he tells a lie, he's doing what comes naturally to him. He's a liar and the father of lies." - John 8:44*

If a pin had dropped everyone would have heard it hit the floor. No one spoke for what seemed like an hour. Finally, the officer-in- charge dismissed me. "We'll let you know what we decide."

Not long afterwards I was called to stand before the battalion commander. "I've come to a decision. I'm sentencing you to thirty days restriction. You can work and go to chow, but you must be in quarters by 1900 hours. On the days you're not on duty and on weekends you'll be assigned duties by your platoon sergeant." I breathed a sigh of relief. I expected a much worse punishment, which is what I deserved. There is no doubt that if I had taken the coward's way out and lied I would have been in a lot deeper trouble. I said a silent prayer of thanksgiving for my father's godly advice. I had also learned that my Heavenly Father could be trusted.

> *"Don't lie to each other. You've gotten rid of the person you used to be and the life you used to live, and you've become a new person. This new person is continually renewed in knowledge to be like its Creator." – Colossians 3:9-10*

chapter twenty-six

A Work in Progress

I had come a long way in my relationship with Christ, but I still had a long way to go. I enjoyed listening to Raul Ries, pastor of Calvary Chapel Diamond Bar, California on the radio. But my respect for him grew tremendously when I found out that he was a former Marine and Vietnam Veteran. What's more, he was involved in martial arts. Now this was the kind of pastor I could follow! I bought some of Raul's tapes and began listening to them. I really liked his style of teaching God's Word.

One night I was at a club with my friends when I heard a familiar voice inside me. "What are you doing here? This is not where you belong." I immediately put down my drink, walked out and I never returned. Never. God's gentle voice was starting to become more powerful than the voices of the world, and that made me feel pretty good. The word quickly got around that ol' Thumper was now a Christian, a "Bible Thumper." I even got the opportunity to lead a fellow Marine to Jesus. All of a sudden, I had a purpose in life. I realized God could use me to have a major and eternal impact in other people's lives. Not long after that I was reading the Bible and I asked the Lord how He wanted me to spend the rest of my life. I told him that any sign from Him would be greatly appreciated. I'm not sure what I expected … maybe a telephone call from God? Or a billboard along the freeway saying, "Victor: sell everything and move to the jungles of Africa." I don't know. I suppose He speaks to people in all different ways. Thankfully my request did not go unanswered.

How about you? Have you discovered your purpose in life? If you have ever said, "There's got to be more to life than this," then you are right! There is more to life! Nothing that the world has to offer will satisfy your longing for significance and purpose. If you have surrendered your life to Christ, then the Bible says that you have the same Spirit of God living in you that raised Jesus from the dead. (Romans 8:11) Get a load of that! That's way more powerful than a Black Belt! God has given us the authority to pray for people and see them healed, to help them out of despair, to bring them the amazing hope of eternal life. This is our purpose and our destiny! Are you living in that destiny? Don't settle for anything less!

Shortly before I left the Marines I found out about Calvary Chapel in Vista, California. I liked spending my free time there. I'd just walk in the door with a big smile on my face and ask them if they needed a little help around the place. A secretary or associate pastor would greet me cordially. "Victor, we're so glad to see you. We need the toilets scrubbed. After that, can you pick up trash in the parking lot?"

My reply was always the same. "I'm on it."

There was no job I wouldn't do because I knew it was for the Lord. I also attended every worship service that fit into my schedule. This lifestyle was a long ways away from the parties and club scene I'd left a short while back. I may as well have been living in a different galaxy. I was like a frog that had been slowly dying on dry, concrete streets, and finally tumbled into the froggy pond. It felt like I was coming home to do that one thing for which I had been created. I was discovering my purpose and mission in life and it sure felt good.

"The Kingdom of God is not just talk – it is power!" – 1 Corinthians 4:20

"Isn't life more than food and the body more than clothes?" –Matthew 6:25

"I can guarantee this truth: Those who believe in me will do the things that I am doing. They will do even greater things because I am going to the Father. I will do anything you ask the Father in my name so that the Father will be given glory because of the Son. If you ask me to do something, I will do it." – John 14:12-14

"You are chosen people, a royal priesthood, a holy nation, people who belong to God." – 1 Peter 2:9

chapter twenty-seven

Leaving My Car at the Altar

One day in church I heard the Lord's voice saying, "Give up your car."

Is that you God? I wondered. Couldn't be. It must be the devil.

"Give up your car," He repeated.

It was God! I couldn't deny that gentle persistent voice.

Not my car! I shouted inside my head. But it was too late.

The Lord had spoken, and I knew what must be done. I was learning to trust God because He always knew what was best. Still this wasn't going to be easy. You see, I had a really cool green Cutlass Supreme with mag wheels and a hot stereo system. I really loved that car. So, did everyone I knew. When I was in that car I played things fast and loose. I'd pull up to Calvary Chapel with a boatload of servicemen. Heads would turn, and people would say, "Here come the Marines." We'd enter the church and the ushers would say, "The Marine Corps section is right over there!" Then we'd sit together in the same pew.

Things would never be the same without my green Cutlass Supreme! But I knew what I had to do.

Just before my separation from the Corps I approached one of the Marines who attended church with me. I told him, "I'm getting out and you're going to need transportation to church. The Lord wants me to give you my car."

You might think that's cruel of God to ask me to give up my favorite car. But He knew I loved it too much. He knew that my hands were clenched so tight on that car that I would never have been able to receive all the other incredible blessings that He was planning to give me. He'll never take something away without giving something better in return.

"Bring the full amount of your tithes to the temple so that there will be plenty of food there. Put me to the test and you will see that I will open the windows of heaven and pour out on you all kinds of good things in abundance." – Malachi 3:10 (GNB)

The guy was stunned. I sold him my beloved Cutlass Supreme for one dollar. He continued to take Marines to church, so in a way the thing I loved most about that car lived on. Giving that car away gave me a great, great feeling.

I started to let my hair grow just before I officially separated from the Corps. I knew that I was pushing regulations, and kept the length hidden under my cover (cap) and tucked behind my ears for inspections, but I didn't think anybody would make a big deal about it because my time was short. Then for the first time in my life I was wrong. (Well, maybe the second time!)

My final day as an active duty Marine came on December 26, 1986. I spit-shined my boots, pressed my uniform and went to the administration building to sign out. There I was, standing at the counter to sign my final paperwork and pick up my separation pay, moments away from completing my service and commitment. As I took my cover off a gunnery sergeant from in back of the room passing through saw me and barked at me. "Hey Marine! That's not a regulation haircut."

"I know," I said respectfully, "but I'm getting out right now."

"No, you're not! Not until you get a regulation haircut."

I couldn't believe what I saw as his audacity to nit-pick my hair! Everything else about me was squared away, but he zoned in on my hair!

"Hey Gunny," I repeated with a tense smile, "I'm right here to sign my papers to get out."

"Not with that hair, Marine." And he dug in to his position.

I could feel the rage against this man building inside of me. One of my buddies grabbed me, took me outside saying, "Kennedy, it ain't worth it."

"I'm gonna break this guy in half!" I spat.

"I told you it ain't worth it. Just go get a little trim."

There's a story in the Bible where God asked Abraham to sacrifice his only son Isaac to God. In the end God stopped him from actually sacrificing his son, but He wanted to see if Abraham was actually obedient enough to do it. Abraham was obedient and in return God blessed him with as many descendants "as there are stars in the sky." Did you know that God has similar blessings in store for you? He'll do it for you... if you only give Him what He wants from you today.

Reluctantly I went to the PX barbershop, still angry about being hassled by the gunnery sergeant. Driving to the barber, I offered a "bullet prayer" to God but strangely enough I noticed that God was beginning to soften my heart. By the time I sat in the barber's chair I actually had a peace that could only come from God.

"I'm getting out today and they won't let me go until I get a haircut," I explained.

"Okay," the barber said. "So, you only want it trimmed a little."

"No. Give me a full regulation Marine Corps haircut," I insisted.

"All right. If that's the way you want it."

The barber did his thing, and then I went back to the gunnery sergeant to do mine.

I went straight back to the administration building, walked past the front counter, and proceeded to walk back to the desk of the gunnery sergeant who gave me grief about my hair. The tension in the room grew with each advancing step I made toward him. Everyone must have thought that "Thumper" was going to blow and the loose cannon was ready to explode!

When I stood in front of his desk I was completely squared away. I put my fists on his desk, leaned forward, and he leaned back.

"Is this regulation haircut satisfactory, Gunnery Sergeant?" "It looks good, Marine," he mumbled.

"Let me tell you something," I said. "Before I would've jumped up and busted you in half for making me get a haircut. But now I'm gonna tell you that I love you, man."

The guy just stared at me. He was obviously surprised.

I continued. "I love you because of the love Jesus Christ has shown me. You were right, and now I can leave the Corps like I should."

He didn't know how to respond. Stumbling he said, "Uh, that's nice. That's great. Okay."

I picked up my papers and left as a civilian for the first time in three years. The Marines had been good for me and I was in a better place than ever before. *Semper Fidelis*. Always faithful. But even better, I was learning to be faithful to God. Because He had been so faithful to me.

chapter twenty-eight

My First Call into Ministry

After visiting my family, I went back to Vista, California, and continued my volunteer work at Calvary Chapel. I had the opportunity to meet Pastor Chuck Smith, whose voice I had become so familiar with on the radio. He shook my hand.

"Well, Victor," he said in his deep, deliberate voice. "I've heard good things about you."

I was surprised that he knew my name. It seemed that someone had been ratting on me. A few days later, Pastor Brian from Calvary Chapel Vista approached me.

"Victor," he said, "we've given it a lot of thought and we want to bring you on staff."

"You mean that, really?" I stammered.

"We want to make you the junior high school pastor." Pastor Brian smiled. "By the way, this is a paid position."

Wow! I'd been looking for a job, but I didn't know that a job had been looking for me!

On the first day of class I nervously waited for my students. We were meeting in a bus because there weren't enough classrooms to go around. That day only two girls showed up and I was so disappointed. But one of them gave her life to Jesus that night, so God turned my disappointment into incredible joy.

In the following weeks I loved teaching the kids Bible stories like David and Goliath because it was all about fighting. I became really animated as I acted it out.

"He whirled his slingshot, the giant slumped to the ground, little David chopped Goliath's head off, the blood was flowing everywhere, what a sight!"

The kids' eyes were popping from their heads as they experienced the Bible from my perspective. And the staff was probably regretting the day I was hired.

Soon I had the opportunity to visit my dad again. I was beginning to think about changing my last name back to Marx. This was not a decision that I took lightly because I had been a Kennedy for most of my life – I'd taken that name from one of my stepfathers. There were certain feelings associated with the Marx family name that I couldn't easily erase. My biological father and I had walked a similar path. We had both reached rock bottom only to have Jesus lift us up to new heights. Our commitment to the Lord was so strong that it couldn't help but overflow into our father-son relationship. Besides, I wanted to show him how much I loved and respected him for what he had done with his life. My change of name would show him how important he was to me.

So, it was settled. I was to become Victor Marx in celebration of my Dad and me coming together in our heavenly Father's presence!

God has an amazing way of bringing people together. Satan's desire is to drive people apart, but God brings them together. He said, "It is not good for man to live alone." (Genesis 2:18) We bring God so much joy when we forgive people who offended us ... when we help bring healing to broken relationships.

Is there a hurting relationship that you can help heal today? I pray that you find joy in all your relationships.

"If we live in the light in the same way that God is in the light, we have a relationship with each other ... Those who love other believers live in the light. Nothing will destroy the faith of those who live in the light. Those who hate other believers are in the dark and live in the dark."
– 1 John 1:7; 2:10-11

[Jesus is speaking] *"I pray that all of these people continue to have unity in the way that you, Father, are in me and I am in you. I pray that they may be united with us so that the world will believe that you have sent me." – John 17:21*

chapter twenty-nine

I'LL MARRY THAT ONE!

I was twenty-one years old by now and the thought of marriage began to cross my mind more frequently. It was as if the Lord was telling me that I needed a partner to go through life with. One Sunday I met a young woman named Eileen Breining. When I first laid eyes on her I immediately cried out to God, "I'll marry that one, Lord! I'll marry that one!" She was drop-dead gorgeous with dark hair, hazel eyes, and beautiful lips. But I also learned that she was not a Christian.

Later at a Sunday morning service a guest singer asked if anyone would like to trust Jesus Christ as Savior. I jumped for joy as Eileen raised her hand. She began weeping as she bowed her head and surrendered her life to the Lord. See, Jesus became her Prince of Peace.

Eileen and I gradually became friends. She invited me out for my twenty-second birthday and she even made me a small cake. Our conversation flowed freely as we spoke about our lives and the Lord. I felt that our relationship was definitely moving to a new level and I was excited about the possibilities. I was already seeing marriage in our future.

The problem was my timing and God's of having a relationship with this beautiful woman... meanwhile....

"Victor, can you give more of yourself to your job?"

"It's just not there anymore," I answered truthfully. "The passion is gone."

The pastor gave it some thought. "What are you good at, Victor? What gives you that passion?"

Thinking it was probably a waste of time, I told him that I was good at karate.

"All right," he responded. "Let's go in that direction."

This pastor really meant what he said. From the pulpit he announced that I was starting a karate class. I was totally shocked when one hundred and twenty people signed up. Within a few weeks I was looking at a class of one hundred and fifty. We had grown too large to hold sessions at the church, so we rented space at a building in town. Then imagine my great surprise when Eileen showed up at the karate class. I heard that Eileen was teaching aerobic classes, so I approached her with an offer.

"Hey, how would you like to teach fitness classes here?"

She already had a full-time job in physical therapy and she was teaching fitness classes at two other health clubs. She told me she would let me know if she could work it out. At the time I didn't know that Eileen was one of the top fitness instructors in America. Soon thereafter, she began teaching classes at my dojo.

Another highlight in our friendship before we started dating was having the privilege of baptizing her in the ocean with our church baptism. Little did I know I was baptizing my future wife and mother of my children. Never be discouraged. God works all things out in His perfect plan and timing.

God showed me that I needed to submit my desire for Eileen to Him. Have you ever had a longing for something that was so strong you could hardly contain it? Longings and desires can be dangerous. Either we control them ... or they control us. The Bible says that we can actually become slaves to our sinful desires. Submitting our desires to God means wanting what God wants more than what we want. Have you submitted all your longings to Christ?

"Everyone is tempted by his own desires as they lure him away and trap him. Then desire becomes pregnant and gives birth to sin. When sin grows up, it gives birth to death." –James 1:14-15

"We take every thought captive so that it is obedient to Christ." – 2 Corinthians 10:5

"Happy are those whose greatest desire is to do what God requires;

God will satisfy them fully! Blessed are they who hunger and thirst after righteousness for they shall be filled." – Matthew 5:6 (GNB)

chapter thirty

A Funny Proposal

I was working at the La Costa Spa and Resort in the summer of 1988 when Brian Wilson of the Beach Boys approached me and said, "I'd like to take private karate lessons from you." So, I gave Brian and his personal assistant a lesson that included various styles of fighting. A few days later I received a phone call inquiring if I would be interested in moving to Brian Wilson's mansion in Malibu. I would be paid a handsome salary in exchange for my karate instructions and, I guess, body-guarding.

Would I?! I thought. This is great!!

My friends were so excited. "Wow! He's one the Beach Boys! You can't pass that up!"

Eileen had just begun teaching her fitness classes at my karate school when I approached her with the news.

"I've been offered a job with Brian Wilson of the Beach Boys. I'll have to move to Malibu, but it will be cool." I was feeling pretty good about this offer.

I'll never forget Eileen's response. "Why would you take it? Did God tell you to?"

Her question stopped me dead in my tracks. Was I taking the job simply because someone famous had asked me? Or was this really the right thing to do?

After consulting with the Lord, I went back to Eileen.

"Thanks for getting in my face about that Brian Wilson offer. God didn't tell me to take it. So, I'm turning it down. It just wasn't meant to be."
So, I told them I couldn't come.

Later Eileen and I were in Lake Arrowhead, California, for a Calvary Chapel conference. This was our first outreach together ministering to youth. We drove to a scenic vista called Strawberry Peak. I plucked a long weed out of the ground and twisted it into the shape of a ring. Kneeling down with the makeshift ring in my hand I proposed to her.

"Eileen, will you spend the rest of your life with me?" Eileen burst out laughing. "You're so funny!"

Not the response most guys would expect to receive for a marriage proposal. But I'm not most guys. So, I went at it again.

"Eileen, I want you to be my wife. Let's grow old together. Will you marry me?"

Eileen took a good look at my face. "You're serious?"

"Completely." I held up the weed ring. "I don't have any money and this is the best I can do for now."

She smiled. Her gorgeous eyes gazed deep into mine. Then came her simple reply.

"Yes!"

I gently slipped the makeshift ring on her finger. Then on December 10, 1988, we were married – with authentic rings – and the rest is history. That episode at Lake Arrowhead was the perfect moment that will forever be treasured in our hearts.

chapter thirty-one

A MIRACULOUS MOMENT

Pastor Brian Broderson conducted the ceremony at Calvary Chapel Vista where I made Eileen Breining my wife. Karl Marx – my dad in every sense of the word – recently had moved out to California from Louisiana and was there to be my best man! Pastor Greg and Cathe Laurie were generous enough to give us a luxurious stay at a La Jolla hotel for our honeymoon.

My bride and I opened the New Life Fitness Center. I taught karate while Eileen conducted aerobic and fitness classes. We really felt as if we were doing what we had been created to do in that time and place. I also continued to be actively involved with Calvary Chapel. We declined an opportunity to teach martial arts and aerobics in Italy because it didn't seem like the right thing for us to do, despite some significant financial incentives.

Soon we were blessed with our first daughter. To supplement our income, I took a day job as a janitor at the San Onofre Nuclear Power Plant, while continuing to teach karate later in the evening. Cleaning toilets wasn't exactly my "life's calling," but I made the most of it by leaving gospel tracts around and tuning the office radios into Christian stations. The employees would tell me they had never seen such clean bathrooms.

"Hey, I'm doing this for Jesus," I told them with a smile.

My dad was hired at San Onofre, too. We were blessed to see a lot of each other since we were commuting to work and going to karate classes together.

Soon I felt called to return to Louisiana to start a new Calvary Chapel on the bayou. This was a major decision since we had established our family and our karate and fitness classes in California. But we eventually pulled up roots and moved to Louisiana.

Eileen and I had a second child – a boy – who was born in our new home. I was so excited to have a son born at home on Bayou Blue. He was a bona fide Cajun boy – my "man cub!" Then when he was only seven weeks old he developed a high fever that the doctor diagnosed as spinal meningitis. The prognosis was not good.

"There are seven chances in ten that your son will die, be deaf, or have severe physical disabilities from this illness," the doctor warned us. "A seventy percent chance."

The words were so harsh and so final. It was as if somebody was going to take our child and there was nothing in the world that we could do to stop it. We felt so helpless, and yet in our hearts we knew that we were not without hope. So, we cried out to the Lord for mercy.

Despite my emotional turmoil, I knew in my heart that God was still in control. While in my car I happened to tune into a Christian radio station – it was actually KAJN, the station where I had worked when I was fifteen. A preacher named R. W. Shambock was talking, and as I listened I immediately

"Today is your day for a miracle!" he said. "A child needs a miracle and God is going to provide that miracle and heal that sick child. You must believe!"

I felt the Lord's presence in my car as if He was sitting right next to me. God was letting me know that he would have mercy on my son. I immediately drove to the hospital where Eileen was maintaining a constant vigil. I told her about this message from the Lord. Then literally a few minutes later the doctor and a nurse came into the room.

"Mr. and Mrs. Marx," the doctor said, "your son does not have spinal meningitis."

"Doctor, that's a miracle!" I yelled.

We took our baby home and in three days God had completely healed him. Don't ever think that miracles can't happen!

I must confess that I was tempted to question God's will in this – even to get upset at Him. But I was encouraged to remember all that God had given me since He had pulled me out of the gutter: my beautiful wife, my daughter, my son, my father, salvation, a purpose in life. Who was I to question the wisdom of God's almighty plan? He never promised us an easy road – that doesn't come until after this short life is over. This was honestly one of the toughest times in my life, but I always knew that Jesus was walking right beside me.

"Even if my father and mother abandon me, the Lord will take care of me." – Psalm 27:10

"Be strong and courageous. Don't tremble! Don't be afraid of them! The Lord your God is the one who is going with you. He won't abandon you or leave you." – Deuteronomy 31:6

---

chapter thirty-two

CALIFORNIA DREAMIN'

One day I called my friend Pastor Greg Laurie, in California. I explained to him my frustrations – how we were seeing people come to the Lord but then they'd move on to other churches. Why wasn't our little church growing?

"Victor, I've always seen you as an evangelist, not a pastor," he explained. "I believe you might be working outside of your strengths."

He was right. I had veered away from my first calling to be an evangelist, which means sharing the Gospel with people who never heard it before. That advice from Pastor Greg was exactly what I needed to hear.

I hung up the phone and told Eileen, "Pack it up, baby. We're going back to California."

Packing up and moving seemed as natural to me as changing my socks. Being married and a father didn't deter me from moving from one place to another. That is what I was so familiar with.

"Hallelujah!" Eileen sang out. "No more roaches. No more mosquitoes. No more snakes or alligators."

I think you can tell that Eileen is a California girl. She didn't need much convincing to return. Then I called my Pastor Brian Broderson and asked, "Where can I go to be of the greatest help?"

"A little town called Lompoc, just outside of Santa Barbara," Brian replied. "There's a small church that could use someone like you."

I told Eileen that there was an opening for me in Lompoc.

"That sounds fine," Eileen said. "It's California!"

So, we bid farewell to the alligators and snakes, packed up our stuff, and moved to Lompoc. I began helping Pastor Mark Galvin in evangelism and children's ministry, but I knew I needed another job to support my family. Mark suggested I return to something familiar – like karate.

"This town is too small to support a karate school," I said. And I knew it was true.

But I didn't have a lot of options, so I decided to give it a shot. Two weeks later I had sixty students. In no time the school was thriving, but more importantly the Lord was using it as an entryway into the Kingdom of God. People were being saved through our witness and our Bible studies. Soon I took a little ragtag karate group to the national championships and we won nearly everything in sight. We saw twenty-five national and world championship titles come out of that school. I sponsored a regional karate tournament and people came from all over the Western States.

God caused this little karate school to be rated in the top five schools in America. I was interviewed by The 700 Club. Like I said: this town was too small to support ... Oh, nevermind!

Things were going great. We lived in a country club area. I drove a 1965 Mustang and had a 32-foot RV. We had money galore. On top of everything, my bride became pregnant and gave birth to our blonde-haired, blue-eyed daughter. Life doesn't get any better than that!

And it didn't. Suddenly the bottom fell out of a cup that was overflowing with success. I was performing a demonstration when I blew out my hamstring. To me it sounded like a gun going off in my head. I didn't want anyone to know I was hurt so I somehow made it over to my dad who was watching.

"Please get me out of here before I pass out."

The emergency room doctor examined me and said, "It would have been better if you broke your leg."

In my normal smart-alecky way, I said, "Well, get a crow bar and break it!"

He laughed and then pulled out a big ol' needle, gave me a powerful painkiller and put my leg on ice. Later, I saw a couple of sports medicine specialists who told me I would never kick again. One week later I was teaching again – I felt pressured to keep working in order to support my family.

Sometimes familiar, although easy, isn't always the right thing to do. We can confuse the way we feel with being the right thing to do. Without realizing it, I was subjecting my own family to a potentially unstable and inconsistent environment. I thank God, He took care of us.

It's hard for us big, strong guys and gals to admit our weaknesses. We act so tough and strong, but the truth is that every human is vulnerable. We all need the Lord's strength and protection to survive. It makes God so happy when we voluntarily humble ourselves and confess that we need His strength.

"My help comes from the Lord, the maker of heaven and earth. He will not let you fall. Your guardian will not fall asleep. Indeed, the Guardian of Israel never rests or sleeps. The Lord is your guardian. The Lord is the shade over your right hand. The sun will not beat down on you during the day, nor will the moon at night. The Lord guards you from every evil. He guards your life." – Psalm 121

I stayed heavily medicated while lying on the floor to instruct my students. I had always thought I could overcome just about anything since I had been through so much junk in my life. But this time was different.

The problem soon moved from my leg to my head. I was diagnosed with severe depression, although I strongly objected to the doctor's diagnosis. I saw depression as a sign of weakness. Gradually I came to grips with my problem, although not without some serious side effects from my prescribed medications, like insomnia. They then diagnosed me with Bipolar Disorder, with anxiety and panic attacks. On one particularly restless night I went to Wal-Mart for plants and I landscaped the entire front and back yards while the family slept. It was a tough time for me, but God was always right there beside me. He would only let me fall so far before catching me. God had everything under control and little did I know that He was about to open up a whole new life for me and my family.

chapter thirty-three

Spinning in Hazy confusion

In August of 1995 we received a telephone call from Hawaii.

"Hey, we saw you on the 700 Club. I'm Deano Ishiki, a youth pastor at Calvary Chapel in Honolulu. You guys need to come over here and start a Christian karate school."

So, Eileen and I went on a second honeymoon for ten days to Hawaii. We met Deano and the rest of the church staff. I was invited to come back a month later with a team of my Black Belts to do a series of martial arts demonstrations. We had such a great response that I was offered an amazing opportunity if I would relocate to the Islands to open a karate school.

Another move. I tried to get several of my black belts to take this incredible opportunity with us. Not one did.

But Eileen and I sensed that this was God's leading, so we put our house up for sale. The California market was slow at this time, but our house sold in one day. We put almost everything we owned on the front lawn and sold it all. Then on November 2 we flew to our new state of residence with 20 boxes left of all our belongings.

I began teaching karate in a small rented facility with one hundred and forty students. Within a year we had over three hundred students and the fastest growing school in Hawaii. I eventually ended up in a 6,000-square foot training center with two stories and 30-foot windows looking out on the water at the busiest intersection in Honolulu. A prominent sign announced in huge letters, "VICTOR MARX ACADEMY OF KEICHU-DO." Even better, we were located beneath the "Spaghetti Factory!" Our school eventually became two schools with a membership of over five hundred students and a staff of 15.

When I stepped onto the floor to teach Karate I was able to put aside my depression and hamstring problems and teach some fantastic classes. But when I wasn't teaching I still struggled with troubling mood swings.

Through Calvary Chapel I met an elderly gentleman named Mr. Moffat who was recovering from open-heart surgery. He lived in a nice area of Honolulu and he needed someone to help him maintain his property. In exchange for that he would provide living quarters at a greatly reduced rate.

We took Mr. Moffat up on his offer. He became Eileen's biggest fan as she homeschooled our children. Every night he played big band music and worked crossword puzzles. He watched "Wheel of Fortune" and the "PBS Nightly News Report" faithfully. His sweet disposition and gentleness were a real blessing in our lives when we needed it the most. We thought we'd be helping him by moving into his home, but, he was the one who helped us.

Besides having to deal with bouts of depression, I was diagnosed with Bipolar Disorder. I sought help through medication, but I was either too irrational or stubborn to reach out to the Lord for the help I really needed. Meanwhile I was allowing bad attitudes and a spirit of self-sufficiency to creep into my life. I was not humbling myself before God and asking Him to be my strength in weakness. My instability was taking a toll on our marriage, and Eileen and I argued often. We sought help through counselors, all the while keeping a good game face.

Part of the problem was that I was too wrapped up in my work, or I was using work for a kind of escape. It prevented me from facing the fact that my spiritual life and my family was slowly falling apart. I felt powerless to change and I began to be plagued by suicidal thoughts. I was supposedly a mature Christian and my life was spinning out of control! 42 visits to a psychiatrist in 12 months...ugh.

Through the haze of confusion and hopelessness I realized that I was trying to have a relationship with God on my terms, not His. I was headed for disaster if something didn't change. Thankfully God was watching out for me.

The Great Physician was about to show me the cure.

Some people spend their entire lives looking for greener grass on the other side of the fence. But wherever they go, there they are. This was my problem when we moved to Hawaii. I had the big job, the nice home, the beautiful state, the "happy" family. So why was my life falling apart? Because stuff is just stuff and it will all turn bitter if we neglect the one thing that really matters.

What is that one thing? It's a loving, healthy, obedient relationship with Jesus Christ. Then healthy relationships with people will follow. If your life feels like it's falling apart, and you don't know why, maybe it's time to strip away all the distractions and focus on the one thing that really matters.

---

chapter thirty-four

CATCHING THE PERFECT WAVE

"Who has a prayer they want to say?" asked my daughter's teacher. She was enrolled in a private Christian school at the time.

My daughter raised her hand. "I do. I pray that my dad will never have to take medicine again."

I had plenty of bottles of Zoloft, lithium, BuSpar, Depakene, and Depakote just to name a few. But my little daughter's prayer was more potent than all of them put together. After my girl offered that prayer, I never took another prescription pill for manic depression - ever! There's no other way to explain my healing. Praise God for the faith of a child!

Meanwhile the Lord was speaking to my heart. He was saying, "You've got to cleanse your mind." I immediately began listening to the Bible on tape. I didn't watch television or listen to music for several weeks. Instead I listened to God's Word. As I focused on Jesus, my perspectives, my insights, and my desires for God and His Word intensified. Meanwhile my worldly desires grew weaker as my spiritual self was strengthened and nurtured. An incredible change was happening in my heart.

"I have treasured your Word in my heart so that I may not sin against you." – Psalm 119:11

Maybe you've heard it said, "You are what you eat." Similarly, your character is defined by the things you fill your mind with. People who feed their minds on trash media and pornography and violence will have damaged character and attitudes that reflect those negative

> *things. But when you fill your mind with God's Word, with songs of praise, with godliness and selflessness, then the fruit of godliness will surely blossom in your life. What are you filling your mind with?*

As I drank deeply of God's Word, it truly became a part of me. One beautiful passage of scripture spoke to my life like nothing else: *Blessed is he whose transgressions are forgiven, whose sins are covered. Blessed is the man whose sin the Lord does not count against him and in whose spirit, is no deceit. When I kept silent, my bones wasted away through my groaning all day long. For day and night your hand was heavy upon me; my strength was sapped as in the heat of summer. Then I acknowledged my sin to you and did not cover up my iniquity. I said, "I will confess my transgressions to the Lord." – Psalm 32:1-5 (NIV)*

My healing really began when I accepted this Scripture as the truth that would embrace me for the rest of my life. Two years passed without a mood swing or a serious bout of depression, so I went to my doctor and said, "God has healed me!"

"Victor," my doctor replied. "God didn't heal you. It's going to come back."

As he scoffed at me, I could hear the Lord's voice deep inside my soul: "You can either believe the word of man or you can believe the Word of God."

"Well, Doc," I said confidently, "I've been healed whether you believe it or not."

I didn't care what the doctor thought ... because I believed God! Nobody on earth could rain on my parade. I left the doctor's office praising God for His miraculous healing power.

In October 1997 I attended an Athletes in Ministry conference in Arizona. I listened to many poignant and touching testimonies to the Lord by professional and amateur athletes. Now this touched a passionate nerve in my spirit. Physically, mentally, and spiritually, I was in complete harmony with everything I saw and heard there. Eileen and I continued to run a highly successful karate school in Hawaii, but something had been missing. Greg Laurie and Raul Ries challenged me to get back into sharing my testimony and preaching. So, I combined karate demonstrations with stories of God's faithfulness, and I soon saw people giving their lives to Jesus once more. God's fruit was becoming evident in my life again and that felt good.

Closer to home, the anger and conflict in our marriage had been replaced by tranquility and serenity. Then a new business opportunity opened up. One of my karate students asked me to become part-owner in his construction company and I accepted his offer. God enabled my income to rise significantly as I combined this new business venture with my karate schools and occasional television and personal appearances. I began to feel like the Oahu surfers who try to catch the perfect wave. I felt as if I had spiritually caught my perfect wave, surrounded by the boundless ocean of the Lord's love.

"Blessed is the person who does not follow the advice of wicked people, take the path of sinners, or join the company of mockers. Rather, he delights in the teachings of the Lord and reflects on His teachings day and night. He is like a tree planted beside streams – a tree that produces fruit in season and whose leaves do not wither. He succeeds in everything he does. Wicked people are not like that. Instead, they are like husks that the wind blows away." – Psalm 1:1-4

In the midst of all this good fortune, the Lord led us to go on a mission trip back to the mainland. My wife and kids and I did karate demonstrations and shared my testimony in several states, and we saw 137 people give their lives to Christ. During this trip Eileen and I talked about moving back from Hawaii. Later Mr. Moffat introduced us to two gentlemen who were affiliated with the Focus on the Family Ministry, located in Colorado Springs. Ron Prentice and Doug Gillquist had flown out to the Islands to thank Mr. Moffat for his support of their organization, and Eileen and I were invited to join their meeting. I was touched by these two men's genuine love and concern for this elderly gentleman. Eventually the conversation got around to what I did for a living. I told them about my karate business and Christian ministry. I had no idea at the time how this impromptu meeting would affect our future.

chapter thirty-five

I COULDN'T MISS THE MESSAGE

In early 2001 I slammed into another obstacle: through over training, repetitive sparring and power spinning hook-kicks, my hamstring tore again, and it was much more severe than the first time. God had brought me a long way in my journey since I first injured my hamstring. Thankfully I didn't struggle with anger and depression like I had earlier. Instead I accepted this trial as a stepping-stone for taking me further along the road where God wanted to take me. I knew that this time it was not me being disciplined for disobedience but rather what the Bible calls being pruned like a fruit tree to bring a greater harvest.

My hamstring was in such bad shape that I could not find a surgeon in Hawaii to do the operation. I eventually found a doctor in Sydney who would do it, so off I flew to Australia. As we left the airport I prayed, "Lord, please confirm to me that I'm in your will." When we arrived at the hospital, the doctor introduced the operating team to me. (I'm not making this up.)

"I'm Dr. Cross," the physician said with a smile. This is Dr. Servant, my assistant from England. The nurse is named Joy. And the anesthesiologist is Dr. Hope."

That's not all. As I was taken to my room I saw an office belonging to Dr. Love. Is that God or what!? He was definitely sending me a message of assurance.

Before the surgery began I prayed aloud for the medical team. When I opened my eyes afterwards, Eileen's smiling face was the first thing I saw. The surgery was a success, but my recovery was complicated by pericarditis, or inflammation of the heart sack. I had contracted a virus, post-recovery. Then another miracle happened and with the Lord's help I recovered from both my hamstring injury and the pericarditis.

I still cringe to think of my hamstring ripping. I hate when that happens! Who doesn't? But you'll have to trust me when I say that I'm also glad it happened. The cool thing about God is that He can turn everything bad into good.

"We know that all things work together for the good of those who love God – those whom He has called according to His plan." – Romans 8:28

It's an amazing paradox. If we allow Him to, He'll take what Satan meant for evil and turn it into something beautiful. (Genesis 50:20) He brings laughter from mourning and beauty from ashes. (Isaiah 61:1-3) The fires that the enemy intended to use to destroy us become the tools to refine us like precious gold. So, if you're suffering, don't run from God. Run to Him and allow Him to bring more good from this than you can even imagine.

That August Doug from Focus on the Family called me on the phone.

"Hi, Victor," he said. "Remember me? I met you and your wife back in January. I'm in Hawaii again and wanted to let you know we feel we may have a great opportunity for you in a position here at Focus on the Family."

My family was living quite comfortably with our karate schools and construction business and I couldn't imagine any offer that would entice us to give it all up. Doug met with us and explained the job. I would represent Dr. Dobson on behalf of Focus on the Family, visiting constituents of the ministry and building relationships.

"How can I do this?" I asked, amazed at the proposal. "I'm just a Cajun guy. A karate man."

Then Doug told me the salary that was even less than I expected, and I wasn't expecting much in the first place. I would also have to travel a lot which would take me away from my family. Honestly, I wasn't much interested in the offer.

Doug wouldn't easily be put off. "Would you and Eileen at least come to Colorado in September and visit us before making your final decision?" I told him I'd think about it.

One night at the Academy when visiting with a world-class black belt, I was sparring when my opponent unexpectedly caught me with a solid body shot that broke one of my ribs. A few days later my face turned a jaundiced yellow, so Eileen rushed me to the hospital. The rib had punctured the bottom part of my left lung and blood had gone into that part! As they prepared me for surgery I took Eileen's hand and said, "Honey, I don't want to go to surgery. Let's pray and make a vow that if God keeps me from going to surgery, we'll serve Him regardless of whatever He asks."

"You are extremely happy about these things, even though you have to suffer different kinds of trouble for a little while now. The purpose of these troubles is to test your faith as fire tests how genuine gold is. Your faith is more precious than gold, and by passing the test it gives praise, glory, and honor to God. This will happen when Jesus Christ appears again." – 1 Peter 1:6-7

"That is why we are not discouraged. Though outwardly we are wearing out, inwardly we are renewed day by day. Our suffering is light and temporary and is producing for us an eternal glory that is greater than anything we can imagine." – 2 Corinthians 4:16-17

We prayed right there. Then the medical staff took me for some tests. As they began prepping me for surgery I felt the Lord's peace. Eileen felt the same thing in the waiting room. I sat up. The pain was gone. Totally gone!

Eileen walked in and I told her, "I'm going to be all right." I called for a nurse and asked her to take out the tubes, so I could go home. The doctors couldn't believe it. They said they must have misdiagnosed my problem. But Eileen and I knew what had happened.

"You didn't make a mistake," I told them. "God has healed me."

I got off the table and went home, praising God for what He had done. A few days later I was driving with my construction partner. I began playing a Christian music CD and praying out loud, "Lord, I'm just going to keep my eyes on you. You are in control."

He asked, "What's that all about?"

"Oh, one of the greatest ministries in the world has offered me a position," I explained. "I don't know what to do."

"It's obvious what you should do," he said. "You got to go where God leads you."

I was taken aback by his response. We were making a ton of money and he had rarely spoken about God before. Eileen and I prayed and asked for the Lord's guidance. Finally, we heard the Lord's voice.
"Just go and visit," God said. So, we did.

chapter thirty-six

A FOOL FOR GOD

Eileen and I were living very comfortably. A beautiful home nestled in a rainforest on the top of a small mountain called Roundtop, overlooking Diamond Head with an incredible view of Honolulu and the ocean. We lacked for nothing. We had an imported Mercedes equipped with a racing package for speed and an Alpha Romeo sports car. Of course, we had a family van as well! I had assured Eileen that we were on track to be millionaires. But here we were flying to Colorado Springs to interview for a job that paid peanuts. How crazy was that?

I arrived in Colorado Springs wearing a pair of slacks and a Hawaiian shirt. That comes from living in the Islands for six years. I called Doug when we arrived. He told me what time I should be there.

"Oh, and Victor ... you'll want to wear a coat and tie."

Coat and tie ... What's that?

I rushed to the nearest mall and bought a blue blazer, a white shirt, and a conservative tie. I laughed when I looked at myself in the mirror.

"Who is this person?" I had a headache and was feeling light-headed because of the mountain altitude. The air was dry with low humidity – not at all like beachside Hawaii. Talk about a drastic change!

I told Eileen, "All I want to do is get this interview over with and catch the first plane out of here!"

At Focus on the Family's headquarters I filled out a questionnaire and put down every goofy job I'd ever held in an attempt to discourage them from hiring me. When I went for my personal interview, executive team members of Focus were waiting for me. Shutting the door behind me, I joked, "You're fired, and you can all leave now." Then the questioning began.

"Where did you get your degree?" one man asked.

"Which one?" I shot back. "I've got six in karate and Jiu-Jitsu." "What qualifies you for this job?" they asked.

"Absolutely nothing," I replied. Everybody looked stunned. The truth can sometimes do that to people. "I'm just a Cajun guy who loves Jesus and karate," I added. "What I do have is common sense."

"I'll take that," a future friend named Al De La Roche said.

I was then asked to share my testimony about the Lord. "I love the Lord," I stated without hesitation. "I'm a pretty simple guy. I teach karate and share my testimony of faith and my experiences with those who are willing to listen. Hopefully I am able to make a difference."

Then I was taken to see Del Tackett, the Executive Vice President to Dr. Dobson at that time. Mr. Tackett had worked for President George Bush Sr.'s Administration (who would later become the architect and teacher of The Truth Project ™) and was a very impressive man. He was articulate and he looked me straight in the eyes when he spoke. After a while he asked, "What do you think so far?"

"I don't know if this is exactly what I want to do," I responded. "Would you care to elaborate?" Mr. Tackett inquired.

"Well, I don't like flying and I don't like being away from my family. I don't like the thin air, dry climate, the snow, and the ice. I like the water and the beach, and besides all that, the salary is considerably lower than what I am making right now."

Mr. Tackett was obviously puzzled. "Then why are you here, Victor?" You'll remember that my dad told me to tell the truth, so I simply told it like it was. "Because I asked the Lord for guidance and He told me to come." As an afterthought I added, "But He didn't tell me I had to take the job."

Mr. Tackett nodded. "How do you think you're qualified for this position then?"

"I'm not qualified. But this much I know: if Jesus tells me to come here, He's going to equip me because His strength is made perfect in my weakness."

Mr. Tackett smiled. "Okay."

My inquisition was over, and nobody had died. Then I ran into one of my questioners in the parking lot on the way out.
"Do me a favor," I said. "Make my life easy and don't choose me. Choose one of the other candidates."

As you can see, I didn't want to go to Colorado. The only reason I was there was because I heard God telling me to go. I didn't understand God's purpose in all of that, but I was going on faith that He saw what I couldn't see.

The Bible says that we should "walk by faith, not by sight." (2 Corinthians 5:7) Once we learn that simple concept of obeying God even when it goes against natural logic, the rest is easy (keeping in mind that God would never ask you to do anything contrary to His Word, the Bible). We simply obey and trust that God will fit all the pieces together, even if we don't understand why until we get to heaven someday.

"These things that I once considered valuable, I now consider worthless for Christ ... This is what I do: I don't look back, I lengthen my stride, and I run straight toward the goal to win the prize that God's heavenly call offers in Christ Jesus." – Philippians 3:7, 13-14

"All these people died having faith. They didn't receive the things that God had promised them, but they saw these things coming in the distant future and rejoiced. They acknowledged that they were living as strangers with no permanent home on earth ... These men were longing for a better country – a heavenly country. That is why God is not ashamed to be called their God. He has prepared a city for them." – Hebrews 11:13,16

There. I'd done my best to sabotage my chances of being hired. As Eileen and I drove away, I could easily think of dozens of reasons why this would not be my best professional move and step in life. But against all those reasons, in my heart I knew that God was telling me that this was where I belonged. What a fool I was for God!

chapter thirty-seven

I LISTENED AND OBEYED

I agonized over my visit to Colorado Springs. I had this feeling that I should call the people at Focus and tell them that I wanted the position. It didn't seem right for them to turn me down just because of the things I'd said while I was there. But I couldn't understand my confused emotions, so I called my dad for his advice.

"Dad, I'm having an anxiety attack. I'm having a hard time trusting God. I know I shouldn't feel that way, but I can't help it. I got so much to lose if I make the wrong decision."

"Son, God loves you," he said. "He's always had great plans for you. He believes in you, and you need to keep believing in Him, even if you don't understand. God would never place anything before you that you can't handle."

The presence of God overwhelmed me as I hung up the phone. I could hear the Lord's comforting voice say, "You can trust me because our relationship is built on love." A huge sense of peace flooded my soul. The next day I called Focus on the Family.

The hardest part of leaving Hawaii was saying goodbye to Mr. Moffat. We all loved him dearly, as if he were a part of our family. Mr. Moffat was a man of faith and conviction. He knew how difficult this transition was for me, but he supported my decision because he knew why I was doing it. I still find it difficult to put into words how much gratitude and love I felt for that man. He was not only my true friend but also my mentor. I left my karate school to close friends and some of the best Black Belts I ever had the privilege of training, Marjie Ledgerwood and Rachel Yasui. Our belongings and van were shipped to the mainland and we boarded a plane to California.

We eventually drove our van to Colorado Springs on December 2, 2001. Soon after, I met with Dr. James Dobson and was thoroughly impressed by him. He has a special gift of making everyone feel important when he speaks to them – especially the children. He welcomed my youngest daughter with the words, "Thank you for allowing your dad to come to work with me in the ministry." And she beamed with pride.

I immediately loved working in public affairs at Focus. God handpicked this job for me, despite all my kicking and screaming. It felt great being around so many God-fearing people. I loved experiencing the wide diversity of the body of Christ, while learning to keep the main thing the main thing, which is Jesus. The mission statement of Focus emphasizes evangelism, which is my calling in life. At that time, they had 1,300 employees, 400 volunteers, and a half million square feet of office buildings on 61 acres of land. The funds donated to the ministry were handled with the greatest care and integrity, and no gift was too small to be appreciated, something I would see and later implement in my own ministry. I had hoped that I would be assigned to Hawaii, but it was not to happen. Instead I was assigned to my old stomping grounds in the Deep South. Little did I know that God was directing my steps to something bigger.

Focus on the Family is dedicated to keeping our nation morally and ethically strong. I strongly supported this cause, having learned the benefits of a healthy family the hard way. Despite all my foot dragging in getting there, I loved my job and the things I was able to accomplish in the Lord's work.

It shouldn't be this way, but some of the biggest hindrances for us moving to Colorado were things that really didn't matter in eternity – like our income, the sunny beaches, and our home. Have you ever heard God asking you to give up something? Maybe possessions or un- necessary responsibilities are tying you up. Maybe it's old habits or sin. It's not easy, is it? But if God is telling you to surrender something, then give it up! He knows what's best for you. Don't let that stuff keep you from the incredible reward at the end of the highway.

"Since we are surrounded by so many examples of faith, we must get rid of everything that slows us down, especially sin that distracts us. We must run the race that lies ahead of us and never give up. We must focus on Jesus, the source and goal of our faith. He saw the joy ahead of Him, so He endured death on the cross and ignored the disgrace it brought Him. Then He received the highest position in heaven, the one next to the throne of God." – Hebrews 12:1-2

---

chapter thirty-eight

IT ALL COMES DOWN TO ONE THING

While working for Focus on the Family, I had the privilege of going into homes and meeting many wonderful people. Oftentimes I would ask them a simple question.

"How would you describe your relationship with Jesus through the years?"

Invariably they would answer, "God has been faithful."

I can relate to that, because through all the time that I have been walking with God He has never let me and my family down.

Before I left for work one day, my youngest daughter at the time handed me an envelope. I could feel the weight of some coins inside. Inscribed on the envelope was simply, "Dr. Dodson."

"Daddy, would you please give this to Dr. Dodson?" She asked. "Yes, ma'am, I will," I assured her.

I went to work and hand-delivered the envelope to Dr. Dobson's office. About a week later I found out that my daughter had enclosed a letter with her coins. It read, "Dear Doctor Dodson, Daddy told me that you had to ask people to leave and they couldn't work for Focus anymore because you don't have enough money to pay them. I'm sorry. I've gathered all my money. It's just a bunch of dimes. It's not much but I am giving it all to you. I hope this helps. I love you." And she signed her name.

It was difficult for Dr. Dobson to see people lose their jobs. He cared deeply about each and every one of his employees and he felt responsible for their welfare. He let me know that he wanted to use my daughter's letter in his next monthly newsletter. Dr. Dobson also wrote a touching note to my daughter. It showed a man holding three balloons. On the balloons he had written, "I Love You." My little girl was tickled pink. We proudly displayed the note on our refrigerator. The smallest gift from the heart can have dramatic and far-reaching effects. It can touch people in ways that we never expect.

One day the broadcasting department asked me to share a few thoughts from the Bible with a group of about seventy people in the Focus on the Family welcome center. I brought some of my martial arts equipment to spice things up a little.

"I hope you don't mind," I began, "but I'm going to give you a little martial arts demonstration."

Everyone thought I was kidding until I asked for a volunteer. A college student came forward and I had him hold a pencil between his lips. I began twirling my nunchucks as if I were about to knock the pencil out.

Suddenly I stopped and wiped the sweat off my forehead. "I get so nervous when I'm doing this."

By that time the guy's knees were really shaking. So, I twirled the nunchucks around a few more times and knocked the pencil right out of his mouth. Then I asked for another volunteer and I split a watermelon on his stomach with a razor- sharp samurai sword.

"Some people call me a martial arts master," I explained, "but the Lord is the real master." I then went on to share my testimony with them.

This audience was a real encouragement to me. At first, I didn't think my story was anything special. But God was using me. I saw many people saved at these kinds of presentations or coming back from being away from the Lord. Gang members, prostitutes, and drug addicts came to faith, and at one service I saw forty people surrender their lives to Jesus Christ. I also began speaking at college campus organizations along with junior high and high school groups.

One of the highlights was a Fellowship of Christian Athletes meeting at the University of Alabama in October 2002. One of my volunteers was a six-foot eight-inch, 310-pound Crimson Tide tackle named Wesley Britt. He was also a leader in the Fellowship of Christian Athletes. I had him point a fake pistol right into my face and in a split-second I took it out of his hand and pointed it back at him.

People are so diverse because that's how God made us. He uses people with all different kinds of talents and skills. At one time I thought all Christians had to look, dress, and act alike. I never would have dreamed that God could use my martial arts skills to help other people, or even to lead people to Jesus. But He has done that in my life! How about you? What are your skills and passions? Did you know that God has a purpose for you that include using your talents to bring Him glory and to make the world a better place? You have an amazingly wonderful purpose in life! Just give yourself to Him and watch what He does with your life. That reminds me of a little boy who gave his little lunch to Jesus – and look what Jesus did with it!

"Jesus looked around and saw that a large crowd was coming to Him, so He asked Philip, 'Where can we buy enough food to feed all these people?'... 'There is a boy here who has five loaves of barley bread and two fish. But they will certainly not be enough for all these people.' 'Make the people sit down,' Jesus told them. (There was a lot of grass there.) So, all the people sat down; there were about five thousand men. Jesus took the bread, gave thanks to God, and distributed it to the people who were sitting there. He did the same with the fish, and they all had as much as they wanted. When they were all full, He said to his disciples, 'Gather the pieces left over; let us not waste a bit.' So, they gathered them all and filled twelve baskets with the pieces left over from the five barley loaves which the people had eaten." – John 6:5-13 (GNB)

You should have seen his eyeballs – they became as big as silver dollars. What thrilled me later about Wesley was that he turned down a Playboy Magazine endorsement because of his Christian witness. Wesley went on to play for the New England Patriots in the NFL. So many incredible people like Wesley made my job at Focus on the Family a real joy.

chapter thirty-nine

COMING FULL CIRCLE

As you may recall, I barely made it out of Jasper High School with my diploma. Well, I was getting ready to attend my twentieth high school reunion in the summer of 2003 when I received a call from a former classmate. "Would you be willing to be the speaker for our reunion?" she inquired. I was honored by the offer and I gladly agreed. Eileen and I had been praying for opportunities to share our faith at the reunion.

Unfortunately, I grew more and more nervous as the hour for my speech drew near. By the time Eileen and I arrived at the Sam Rayburn Country Club I felt like I was going to throw up. Eileen had never seen me so torn up before a speaking engagement. The atmosphere there was so strange – like déjà vu, with music from the 1980s and dancing and many boozing up at the bar. What a journey I'd taken since I was last in this place!

Finally, I was invited to come forward to speak. I walked to the front, wondering what I had gotten myself into.

"Hi," I said.

Nobody paid any attention.

"Hello everybody!" I yelled.

There was still no acknowledgment of my existence. I pulled out one of my martial arts swords and started to perform. Nothing like swinging a sword around to get people's attention. Do not try this at home!

"I don't know if any of you remember me," I said. "I was Victor Kennedy when I went to school here. My name is Victor Marx now. This was my fourteenth different school. My mother had been married five times. I had lived in seventeen houses. My father was a drug dealer and a pimp." I then told my former classmates about some of the major events of my life – how I had been molested and locked in a cooler. How God had rescued me so many times that I'd almost lost count. I told them about the letter I'd received from my dad while I was in the Marines, and how I had given my life to Jesus at his church. Then I spoke about the cross on which Christ had died and how He had made all the difference in my life. And I told them about the impact He could have in their lives too.

"I hope my message has encouraged you," I said in closing, "and I'd like to pray for any of you who want prayer."

To my surprise everyone applauded, and many came up to talk to me. Someone said they planned to contact our old principal to tell him how much I had changed. One lady said, "Victor, you've shown all your friends here who the real source of life is, and it's Jesus."

When Eileen and I left, we rejoiced in the incredible victory that God had won that night. But not just that night. God had done a miracle in the life of this boy who had barely graduated from high school. And nobody could rejoice in that miracle more than me.

chapter forty

AN OPEN HEART

During one of my speaking trips I went to Hattiesburg, Mississippi. I felt the leading of God's spirit to go visit the house where Mr. K. had terrorized my family thirty years earlier. I knocked on the front door and an elderly woman answered. I told her who I was and that I had lived in her house when I was a child. She invited me in. I saw the small window through which my family had escaped. Then with tears in her eyes she told me, "When I moved in, I found a box of your family's pictures that was left behind. I kept them for years and prayed many prayers for you children to grow up and know Jesus and to serve Him."

The box of photos was left behind by Mr. K. He probably thought it was just a bunch of useless pictures of our family. He didn't care to take them with him.

Suddenly this woman wasn't the only one in tears. I wondered how many times that little woman was praying in that old house just when I needed it most. I can only imagine.

We had a sweet time of fellowship, that tiny spiritual giant and me, and we ended our time in prayer. I drove off with praise to God in my heart for answering that woman's prayers. I thanked God for leaving those pictures behind, so she could be reminded to wrestle in prayer for our family's deliverance. What a wonderful testimony of God's power and grace!

Again, by the Lord's leading I went to visit Mr. K., who was now over seventy years old. I called him on the phone and he gave me directions to where he was living in Jackson, Mississippi. I drove down a dirt road near a fishing camp and found his little trailer. He gave me a nervous greeting. He was obviously apprehensive about why I wanted to see him. I suggested that we go for a cup of coffee and, so we ended up at a little café in town.

"Two weeks ago," he told me, "I was in a bar and got into a fight. I broke a guy's jaw."

I could see that not much had changed.

Then his conversation took a strangely different direction. "I was never faithful to your mother. Women and alcohol consumed most of my life. That's just the way it was."

That was his way of telling me he was sorry, and I accepted it from the bottom of my heart. As we drove back to his trailer, I sensed that the Lord was speaking to me. He was telling me to give him one hundred dollars, although I really needed the money myself. I had babies at home who needed diapers, milk, etc.

I pulled out the bills. "I want you to take this." "You don't owe me nothin', boy!" he said.

"I know, but I got it and the Lord is telling me that you can use it. That's good enough for me."

As he took it, tears ran down his cheeks. "Victor," he said, "I didn't know if I was going to have anything to eat tonight. Thank you."

I visited Mr. K. several times and I shared my commitment to the Lord with him. Not surprisingly I learned that he, too, had suffered through some serious childhood rejection. Then in June of 2003 my sister called and said that he was very sick. When I arrived, he was in extreme pain and unable to walk. We took him to a hospital where he was diagnosed with advanced terminal cancer.

Over the next few days I visited him while he was in the hospital. With everything the doctors said, it looked like his time on earth wasn't going to be much longer.

One night after a visit to him at the hospital, I woke up at about 4:00 A.M. and couldn't go back to sleep. I felt a real burden for Mr. K. and I started praying for him. Even though this man had done such harm to me as a kid, which resulted in so much emotional and psychological pain over the years, I just couldn't face the fact that if he died and he wasn't saved, he was going to hell for eternity.

I cried out to the Lord, asking Him to not let Mr. K. go to hell. I wanted him saved. My prayer turned to sobs and I cried uncontrollable tears to God on his behalf. I could only explain this by saying that the Holy Spirit filled me, and I was interceding for a soul, no longer my abuser.

The next day, in his hospital room I asked Mr. K. if I might read some verses from the Bible to him. He gladly agreed. We held hands and I prayed.

He proudly introduced me to the medical staff. "This is my son. He's a preacher man. And I'm proud of him. He's worried about my eternity. But he doesn't have to worry any more. I made it right with God last night."

I really do love martial arts, and looking back I can see how that passion grew out of the horrible abuse I suffered as a child. Here's why: The reason I got involved in martial arts – and the Marine Corps, for that matter – was because I didn't want anybody to hurt me anymore. At the time, I figured that if I couldn't beat them with my hands, then I could at least shoot and kill them. Those things gave me a huge sense of control. I already told you how I was walking a dangerous line there for a while, before I surrendered to the Lordship of Jesus Christ. I might have killed somebody and gone to prison for the rest of my life. But thankfully God got a hold of me before that happened. He redeemed me and gave me the beautiful Fruit of the Spirit.

Last night?! I knew then, that I had in prayer been part of the spiritual battle for his soul.

When we left I told him that I loved him, and he turned, and he looked at me and said, "I love you too, boy!"

And in that moment in the hospital I heard him say the two things I had never heard him say to me, but as the only dad I really knew growing up had wanted to hear, despite the abuse: that he was proud of me, and that he loved me.

I knew that I would never see him in this world again. This incredible story would have never been possible if the Lord had not given me an open heart to forgive him. Thanks to God I was able to share some precious time with a person who had held an important part in my life, who had now made it right with God. This was truly a miracle.

My little Cajun mother still lives in Jasper, Texas. She too has overcome a painful past and is looking forward to a glorious future. She studies her Bible and stands boldly in her commitment to the Lord. I am proud to call her my Momma. She is one of the most committed prayer warriors that I have ever known!

My Dad, whom I formerly called Karl Marx, resides in Santa Maria, California. He's an ordained minister through Calvary Chapel. He is remarried to a wonderful Christian woman, Kathleen, and has two grown sons. It's great to see how God has given Dad a chance to be the type of father that he had always hoped to be. I'm proud to say that my Dad is a Tenth Degree Black Belt and a Grandmaster who oversees many of his Keichu-Do karate schools scattered throughout the United States and abroad. He still teaches karate well into his seventies and continues to produce national and world champions.

My dad and I had the opportunity to conduct a mini-crusade together at Mountain Springs Christian Church in Colorado Springs in October of 2003. We also performed karate demonstrations before a crowd of people. To share this experience with my dad meant a lot to me. The power and presence of God was intense as more than one hundred people surrendered their lives to Jesus there. Then my dad tested my son's skills in karate and actually knighted him as a First Degree Black Belt at a special ceremony. Our family now includes four generations of self-defense experts. My grandfather was a professional fighter and self-defense expert. My dad, as I've said, is a Tenth Degree Grandmaster Black Belt. I'm a Seventh Degree Black Belt, and now my oldest son is a Second Degree Black Belt. Dad took a sword and placed it on both of my son's shoulders, then I washed his feet and Dad dried them with a towel. Symbolically, we were saying that being a servant of God is more important than being ranked high in martial arts.

"What human nature does is quite plain... People become enemies and they fight ... But the Spirit produces love, joy, peace, patience, kindness, goodness, faithfulness, humility, and self-control. There is no law against such things as these." – Galatians 5:19-23

Today I advise young people who are coming out of abusive situations first to surrender their lives to Jesus, who is the only one who can heal them emotionally and spiritually. They need to be empowered by the Holy Spirit and live with the Fruit of the Spirit in their lives. Secondly, they really need some good counseling. (Dr. McDonald has more to say about that in the appendix.) Then I also recommend that they get involved in something that empowers them, like self-defense classes, or martial arts, or sports. I think that involvement helped me not to become an offender myself, because so many people who were molested grow up to hurt other people. God is so merciful! He turns anger and hate into peace and love!

"Above everything, love one another earnestly, because love covers over many sins." – 1 Peter 4:8

---

chapter forty-one

ALL THINGS POSSIBLE

After working at Focus on the Family I went on to establish a ministry called All Things Possible, where I continue to speak using martial arts and sharing my testimony to lead people to Jesus. It's crazy how I got into this new ministry. It all started on a "date night" with my bride in 2003. We were leaving a mall in Colorado Springs when a carload of rowdy gang-bangers pulled up next to us with the music blaring. Well, I knew they were no match for an old guy and his wife who was eight-months pregnant in a minivan, so I yelled for them to pull over and meet me in the parking lot.

These gentlemen were ready for some action, so we stood nose to nose there on the pavement. Eileen knew how crazy her ADHD husband of fifteen years could get, so she just sat and prayed. I told them about how I was a martial arts master. I told them that the current reigning United States National Karate Champion was a young man whom I had trained named Jeff Crothers. They didn't seem much interested until I told them that I had seen an illegal weapon in their car at the stoplight. It was a Balisong or Butterfly knife. Somehow, I convinced them to get it for me (they had stashed it under the back seat), and they were fairly impressed by my demonstration of twirling, flipping, opening, and closing the knife faster than a switchblade.

As Eileen continued praying in the van, I sensed that the Holy Spirit was about to do something powerful. God allowed me to share some of my past and tell them the story about the real Master, Jesus Christ, and what He had done for them on the cross. Miraculously three of the four youths actually let me pray for them standing right there in the parking lot as they responded positively to the message of God's grace. Praise God for the work He did in these boys' lives! But the fourth youth was a real tough case. His big hair waved wildly in the air as he spewed filthy profanities in my face. Then he started attacking Jesus and the Bible. He screamed that there was no way that God could be a loving Father. He had lived through fifteen years of hell, and gang life was the best that this world has to offer. He was so angry. It was as if he was possessed. The other guys actually had to physically restrain him to keep him off of me. I could only leave this young man with the promise of a future and a hope, if he would only receive God's loving plan for his life. (Jeremiah 29:11) The others apologized for his behavior and they thanked me for taking the time to share with them. We then slapped hands (the street way) and said goodbye.

End of story? No way! Fast-forward three months to when I was asked by a Christian brother to come to a youth prison and share my testimony and some martial arts. Seventy-five youth sat in that facility, and sitting in the very back row was that angry big-haired kid. You bet I was shocked and amazed to see him sitting there! But this was no surprise to God.

I went on to perform a weapons demonstration in which I unfortunately hit my assistant in the chin with the nunchucks. Whoops! This guy bled profusely and yet allowed me to take another swing and knock the pencil out of his mouth. Needless to say, I had the full attention of everyone. Then I went on to share about the goodness and faithfulness of God. When I gave these hurting youths an opportunity to receive forgiveness, fifty-three of the seventy-five stood to show their desire to follow Jesus!

Naturally I had my eye on one particular kid in that room. Well, I can hardly find words to express the joy in my heart when that big-haired gang-banger kid surrendered his life to Christ Jesus!

Then I walked to his side. "Hey! Do you remember me?" "Yeah."
"Why today?" I wondered.

I will never forget what this old man of sixteen years said. "Mister, I am tired of living my life on my own and you said Jesus could help me." And that, my friend, is why we do what we do. That was the beautiful birth of this ministry called All Things Possible – because miracles are truly possible today!

Eileen and I now have five wonderful children and God has blessed us so much. I've had many close calls and horrific experiences, but God has used many of them for good in the end. "We know that all things work together for the good of those who love God – those whom He has called according to His plan." (Romans 8:28) I am strong today because in my weakness I cried out to God. "My grace is all you need because my power is made perfect in weakness." (2 Corinthians 12:9) I'm a walking miracle, with no credit to me. God gets all the glory!

A Christian counselor once told me, "In 30 years of practice, I never met anybody with as horrible of a childhood as yours." People say it's a miracle that I didn't do what so many other abused and tortured kids do: they go ballistic with rage, they kill people, they kill themselves, some develop same-sex attractions (SSA), or they become abusers and molesters themselves. They spend years trying to numb their pain with drugs or alcohol or anger or sex or other destructive coping mechanisms. But thankfully like Joseph in the Bible, I can say to the devil, "Even though you planned evil against me, God planned good to come out of it. This was to keep many people alive, as he is doing now." (Genesis 50:20) By God's grace, the things that Satan intended for destruction have become a springboard to give higher glory and praise to God today.

God did not miraculously deliver me overnight. In earlier times I suffered from rage. I wanted to take my own life or kill others. I struggled with post-traumatic stress disorder, but through prayer and Biblically based counseling I have found healing. It's a journey and I'm not saying it's over, but I thank God that I have not had any desire to become a sexual offender. For me sexual things were always very sacred and holy – this is a miracle of God in my life. For me the spiritual and emotional healing that God has accomplished was a slow and at times painful process. But don't be discouraged if you are fighting that battle now, because it's definitely a battle worth fighting. All things do turn out for good when we surrender our lives to Jesus. (Romans 8:28) If you are still struggling with issues of past abuse, then hopefully Dr. McDonald's words in the appendix will take you further along in the healing process.

When I was a boy, my family rescued me from a commercial cooler and placed my unconscious, nearly frozen body in the sun's rays to thaw me out. As I grew older and found my soul being drugged to sleep by sin, Jesus placed it before the warming rays of His love. I watched Him bring me back to life. My spirit is now fully awakened because of Jesus Christ's death and resurrection on the cross.

I have learned to trust Jesus and believe what He says. "Whom the Son sets free, he is free indeed" (John 8:36). He has set me free. I live each day with an expectant excitement of what incredible things God is going to do in the lives of the people He brings before me as I share of His great love and faithfulness.

If you are still asleep … then awaken and live life as you have never known it before. Call out to Jesus today! Receive His Peace, His Purpose, His Power, and His Presence!

God bless you!

chapter forty two

RELUCTANT BUT WILLING...

Not long after Victor got back from spending 30 days in the jungles of Burma with Dave Eubank, I received a call from a friend who is a Middle Eastern gal with whom we had done ministry together. She let us know she was going to Iraq to take clothes to people who were chased, brutalized, and forced out of their homes by ISIS earlier that year. These people had to flee for their lives to the mountains with very few belongings and certainly not enough to protect themselves from the cold mountain climate.

Our conversation continued and what she said next brought such sobriety to my heart it was difficult to hear the rest. She told me hundreds of young women who had been kidnapped by ISIS were now free. However, the evil they had endured as captives, including being sold repeatedly to different ISIS members, has led many of these young women who were now free to kill themselves. The trauma they endured was too much for many of them and the only way they knew how to handle it was to take their own life. She said, "They need help with the trauma."

Right after that phone call I told Victor, "We've got to help them!" He said, "No, we can't help. I just got back from Burma!" I knew it seemed crazy to even ask him.

The next week I called and emailed different ministries that I thought might be able to help. I contacted psychologists I knew and told them about what was happening in Iraq with these young women. Sadly, I received no response from anyone. I was very frustrated with those who had the training and understanding of trauma but had no interest in helping. I couldn't blame them. Who, in their right mind, would want to go to Iraq with all the horrible things being done to those whom ISIS considered infidels, and Americans were high on their list.

My next option was to press into Victor again and tell him we must do something. Again, he said "No." I asked him, "Did you pray about it?" Right then, he heard the Lord say, "You need to do this." When Victor heard that he knew it was the Lord and got on the phone and started recruiting a team of trauma specialists to go with him to help these young women. Within a matter of weeks, he had his team willing and ready to go on this High Risk Mission. He had his trauma team, chaplain, worship leader and a 5-man Tier One Security Team.

What happened next made Victor very uncomfortable and very reluctant. I had sensed the Lord wanted me to go to simply love on these young women. I told Victor that I was sensing the Lord wanted me to go with him. He was adamant and said, "No, you cannot go."

Once again, I asked him to pray about it. He asked me why I would want to go and risk my life for these young women? I told him, "When you go and find these young women, in their culture, a man cannot hug these women, but I can." He didn't know what to say. But for the next 10 -14 days he kept showing me images of horrible things that were happening to women over there. He showed me videos of ISIS social media designed to instill fear in people all over the world. These images were indeed very horrific and anyone in their right mind would say, "No way!" Well, despite all of that, I felt God's peace and protection over me.

February 22, 2015, there I was with Victor, his trauma team and security team, on our way to Northern Iraq. We had a total of two weeks to meet with and bring as much help as we could to these once held captive young women.

Upon our arrival, we were given a schedule of meetings that put us before Government officials, Parliament members, doctors, and pastors, all who were completely overwhelmed by the incredible number of people who had been chased out of their homes and villages by ISIS and were now seeking refuge in their cities.

They shared that since ISIS started killing, kidnapping, and causing people to flee there were now over a million people (Yazidis, Christians and even Muslims) who had come to their region of Kurdistan to find refuge. In talking with the officials, they were the ones who were helping to get these young women back from ISIS.

Finally, after days of meetings and interviews with many of the Kurdistan leaders and many local news stations (all wanting to know why this group of Americans would come here to help), we were finally able to meet the young women.

I thought I was prepared to see these young women and just love on them. After the first day of sitting down and listening to their stories I was feeling so incredibly overwhelmed with sadness and grief for them that it was hard to hold in my emotions. Sitting and listening to a young woman, 20 years old, I thought this could have been my own daughter. She started telling me how she escaped ISIS. One night, during a U.S. airstrike, she saw her opportunity to run while ISIS members were engaging in retaliation. She ran into the street and found a taxi driver who had compassion on her and brought her home where his wife could take care of her. This man (an angel) could get her to her home in Sinjar. When she got there, she found out that all the men in her family had been killed and that all the other older family members had been put in a barn and gasoline poured all over them. One of the ISIS members was preparing to light them on fire but received a phone call and left. Her mother was in that group of people in the barn. I lost it right there and started crying, feeling so much pain for her. I looked at one of our trauma specialists and she lovingly gave me a look that said, "Hold it together Eileen, we will have time to cry later." I recovered my composure, continued to listen to these young women and just hugged them and in English told them how much God loved them. I knew they couldn't understand me, but I wanted to speak that truth out loud. Our team was able to spend a couple of days with these amazingly brave young women. We took them to lunch, shopping and gave them what was needed at that time. There were so many tragic stories that they shared, that I can truly say I understood how, without help or hope, many young women like these took their lives. Incredible trauma, indeed, was what these young women had endured.

We also had the opportunity to go into several of the IDP (Internally

Displaced People) camps. Thousands of people were living in each camp. While driving to the camps, from a distance, you could see the seas of tents lined up in rows, tons of garbage on the side of the roads, children running around and adults sitting outside their tents. "What kind of a place is this to live?" was running through my head as I was seeing all this. As we got out of the vehicles the children swarmed around us. They saw we had things in our hands and wanted whatever it was. We had brought beanies (hats), blankets, gloves, scarves, and candy. These children were so happy to see us. Many of the older siblings were carrying their younger siblings on their hips while they received a gift. Once again, the sight of all these children was overwhelming. So much need and so little help.

While visiting another camp, Victor met with a gentleman who was a pharmacist and had been blessed with wealth and a large family. When ISIS came through his town he and his family fled. He was now living in an IDP tent while some of his daughters were still held captive by ISIS. He privately shared with Victor and started to weep when talking about his daughters. He was the leader of his family and felt helpless to provide for and rescue his captive children. Victor prayed for him and gave him some money to take a little burden off this desperate father.

For another group of these people we visited, we had a box full of little stuffed lions and lambs. We had only 25 of each. A donor sent those to us before we left and wanted us to give them out. As we began handing these out, to our surprise, not just children were reaching for one, but older women as well. I was disappointed we didn't have more because these simple little stuffed animals brought smiles and comfort to those who received one.

Victor was invited to the front lines with a couple of his security guys and team members. While out there he was introduced to many of the leaders of the brave Peshmerga fighters. At that time, they were holding down 70 miles of land preventing ISIS from being able to cross into Kurdistan. It was a very serious situation trying to keep ISIS fighters at bay. Victor was able to cross the language barrier and bring some encouragement and laughter to these fighters. He made them laugh and listened to their concerns about this whole situation. I don't think that Victor realized it at the time, but I believe God was developing relationships between Victor and the Peshmerga for future visits. During the earlier meetings, Victor had met with the Ministry of Defense, Generals, and many other key leaders in the region. He was invited to come back and help.

Our time went by so fast. Before we knew it, we were on the plane heading back to the U. S. Then, back in the states, both of us had this overwhelming feeling that we must do something. Our video team had captured footage and made powerful videos to help us show the world what is really happening in Northern Iraq. With firsthand knowledge of the complete devastation caused by such evil, and so many innocent children suffering, we felt God was wanting us to do more.

Before long, Victor was heading back, this time with a few pastors who had heard about all that ISIS was doing, and they wanted to see for themselves. Once again, God had opened doors for Victor to meet some very special people. One little 8-year-old girl who had been held captive by ISIS for the past 7 months was jumping around smiling, but Victor knew that this little girl had been through unbelievable abuse, and, as a little girl, she didn't know what all that meant. Victor knew and was so very grateful to have met her and to know that she was free. He also knew she would have struggles later in life trying to process all that had happened to her.

Another young woman, 15 years old, had severe burns on her face, arms, and hands. She had been turning on the kerosene stove in her camp tent and the kerosene exploded. She was in such pain and as Victor was talking to her, her father was shooing away flies from her. Victor asked what she would need to get better. The father told him she needed more surgeries. Victor asked how much it would cost to get her better. Her father told him $2500. Victor said, "I will be back." He called me and told me what was going on, and asked me to wire the funds over to him. Through a shout-out on our social media, $4500 came in! Victor walked back into her tent the next day and laid the $4500 out on the bed for the father. He actually told his daughter that he didn't really expect that Victor would return as he had promised and so was very surprised to see him bringing the promised funds to help them.

Victor's heart was being drawn to help these people and it was obvious that God was going before him opening doors of opportunity to do just that. Not only were many individuals being helped, but families, Christian families, that were fleeing ISIS were now in Victor's sights.

An amazing story I must share here. One of the trips Victor made back to Northern Iraq was to meet with a very influential Sunni Muslim leader. This man (Victor called him "The Professor") had wanted to meet with Victor because he had learned all that Victor was doing to help people there. One night, after one of the meetings, it was time for the Professor to go the mosque and pray. Victor, being very adventurous, asked if he could go with the Professor. "Yes," was the reply. This was a pretty risky move for Victor and his security team who had to accompany him but Victor had God's peace. As Victor entered the mosque and saw the men praying he felt conviction. He could see how genuine these people were and so faithful to their religion, that he said he wished he had more discipline to meet with God, more one on one, not because he should but because he wants to. While the Professor was praying, Victor and one of his security guys started praying quietly the blood of Jesus over them; that the Holy Spirit would come down and do an amazing work that only He can do.

I believe the Professor was moved at Victor's gesture to want to attend his prayer time with him, because the next day the Professor took Victor to a church building where 12 Christian families were living after fleeing from ISIS. The Professor told Victor, "These are your people, can you help them?" Both Victor and Jack, (his security guy), felt so moved by not only what the Professor asked, but also at the plight of these families. Not long after that, all these families were relocated to apartments (one for each family) in a safe location. That was made possible with donations by people across the U. S. who had been informed of what these families had gone through.

Victor keeps in touch with the Professor. In fact, another amazing opportunity came up for Victor to be a light to show the Professor that not only did God love him completely, but that Christians across America love him too. The Professor needed surgery on his knees but was unable to have this done. Victor let him know that he and many other believers in the U. S. wanted to help him pay for his surgery. The Professor was very humbled and grateful at this news. The interesting thing was that he had access to millions if not billions of dollars through people he knew, but he couldn't take their money as he knew it wasn't 100% clean money. So, God provided for this Professor to have not only one knee repaired but both knees! Christians all over the U. S. made this possible through their selfless donations.

Back in the states, my mind was going back to the small group of children and the simple joy they had when they received a little stuffed lion or lamb. Knowing the tens of thousands of children living in these tents, we wanted to do something more, something that would bring comfort and peace to their hearts and minds. We wanted to let them know just how much God loves them and cares deeply for them. Learning about the culture they live in, trying to spread the Gospel outright would be offensive and would prevent us reaching and helping them. The last thing we wanted to do was close this door that God had opened. We had the thought of putting calming music along with prayers in their language inside little stuffed lions and lambs. We knew that not only the child but also their family members would be able to hear the music and the prayers. After much research, finding the right manufacturing company, 12 months of telling folks how they could help us put one of these healing toys into the hands of the children, our new team went back to Northern Iraq and hand-delivered 11,000 of these little Lions and Lambs. Such beautiful faces and smiles made it worth it all. Our only regret with that trip was that we didn't have enough for all the children in the camps.

As I write this, our family just returned to the U. S. from spending the summer in Northern Iraq where we delivered another 10,000 Lions and Lambs and our teams are still there handing out thousands more. In addition to being able to hand out these Lions and Lambs, we also had backpacks and a comic book of Victor's testimony story along with a band-aid kit for cuts and scrapes. Once again, the children are our focus, as we know their hearts and minds need to hear hope and that they are cared for and loved.

During our time there with our two younger children who are 12 & 13 years old, Victor went out to Mosul a few times to help deliver baby food, water and diapers to the families still fleeing from ISIS. He and his team spent a lot of time with General Mustafa, an Iraqi General who witnessed Victor's care for the innocent children.

General Mustafa invited us (our entire team) to his house when he was on a short leave. His gracious wife cooked an amazing table of Iraqi food. I think there were a total of 10 different servings of food. We were bursting at the seams but so blessed to have such beautiful hospitality. Before the evening ended, the General heard that it was Victor's birthday soon.

He and his son took me aside and said they wanted to help me with a birthday party for him. They chose a popular restaurant which serves large groups of people. The next day all of us joined the General and his family for a wonderful birthday celebration. They had fireworks prepared for when Victor got out of the car, balloons, music, and a birthday cake with an image of Victor's book cover that had Happy Birthday Victor! These people mean business and they also eat cake before dinner!

The General and his family are of the Muslim faith and they know that we are Christians. They presented a beautiful silver cross as a birthday gift for Victor. We were so surprised that they would give him such a meaningful gift. The General had told Victor earlier, "You and Dave Eubank have shown me as well as my men what it looks like to be a Christian by how you treat and care for people." All Victor could say was, "Thank you."

The General was back on duty and soon Victor received word saying there was a baby boy whose parents had been shot as they were being liberated from ISIS.

A brave Iraqi soldier went after him and he too was shot and killed. They named this little baby "Ali" after the soldier who rescued him. To our delight, Victor went back to Mosul and brought back baby Ali to us. We cared for him until a relative could be found. This sweet little baby boy, maybe 11 months old, was so full of joy. He captured our hearts and will always stay in our hearts and minds. His grandmother was located and he was reunited with her a week later. It was bittersweet for our family when Victor had to turn him over to her.

We also had the privilege of caring for the little girl who was hiding under her dead mother's hijab for 2 days, coming out only to get water after her mother was shot and killed by ISIS as they were fleeing. This little one was known all over the world across all media as "The Girl with No Name". Dave Eubank, backed up by General Mustafa and the Iraqi military rescued her under direct fire from ISIS. She became very famous and made headline news over her horrific experience. She was under the General's care and he contacted Victor again to see if he could help get her medical care. When Victor met her, she was very lethargic and non-emotional; her little spirit was simply crushed. She took to Victor and allowed him to hold her. To our surprise, over the next few days, our two children were able to make her smile and laugh by blowing bubbles. Scout, our security dog, also got her to smile. She won our hearts, especially Victor's, as the next few times she saw him, she would light up and want him to hold her. She has been reunited with her aunt who also provided her name, Demouah, which in Arabic means 'tear' and we understand she is doing very well.

I must share one more story of when General Mustafa contacted Victor and let him know of another little baby girl who was pulled out of the rubble. Both her parents had been shot and killed after being liberated and fleeing for freedom. This little girl had no known relatives but needed care. Victor and his team went back to Mosul and picked up this little one and brought her back to our team house. She was so tiny, very malnourished, and so fragile. We didn't know her name but, since she looked like "Boo" on Monsters Inc., we started calling her "Boo." One of the saddest things for me to witness as a mommy was when we gave her a bottle of formula she didn't know how to suck on it. It took her awhile to get the hang of it and when she did, she gobbled up two cans of formula within days.

After a few days with her, getting her medical treatment, bugs out of her hair and filling her with good nutrition, we got word that her older sister was found! That night her sister was brought to us and while little Boo was sleeping, her sister climbed in bed with her. In the morning when Boo woke up, she had her big sister right next to her. The joy on both of their faces was imprinted on our hearts. We are happy to report that their relative was located and they both were reunited with them in the next few days.

Today, from the horrors of what ISIS has done, there are so many children who are now orphans. It became obvious that God had opened another door for ATP Ministries. This time to open a much-needed orphanage in Northern Iraq. We are calling it the ATP Mercy House. We began the process of funding for 2 separate orphanages in Iraq. The first orphanage to provide immediate shelter on a smaller scale. At this writing, this new home, organized by a local Iraqi family, is already under construction. It will provide safe housing to 12 orphans, and/or widowed mothers with children. ATP sought to raise $20,000 for this project, and gracious donors caught the vision and fully funded this first orphanage. The second ATP Orphanage will require long term funding. The hope is to build a large scale orphanage and care center in a safe and secure location in Iraq. This shelter will provide security, aid, and trauma treatment for dozens of people including orphans, human trafficking survivors, widows and others affected by ISIS.

Our hearts are for children here in the states as well as Northern Iraq who, beyond their control, have become victims of abuse, tragedy, and pain. These are the innocent ones who God tells us to take care of. As we have the opportunities and needed support, we will be able to reach, restore and bring hope to the least of these.

What would you do if you were standing right next to an ISIS Commander who was just captured? Well, Victor had the opportunity to talk with this ISIS Commander who once had power and most likely authority to kill and commit evil acts on innocent women and children. He was now sitting on the ground with his hands tied behind his back, with a Belgium Malonois looking intently at him as Victor was speaking to him. Victor, understanding this man had committed such atrocities against who knows how many people, was now looking at the end of his life. I believe Victor had mixed emotions for him. He began asking him questions, (through an interpreter). He asked him, "Do you know what's going to happen to you when you die?" He said "No." Victor then let him know, in a very matter of fact tone, "You know you most likely won't be here much longer."

Victor then shared about the confidence that, when he dies, he knows with all his heart that he will go to heaven because of what Jesus did on the cross for him. Jesus is, in fact, the Son of God, who came from heaven to earth to reconcile God and man. The only way to get to heaven was by believing in that work that Jesus did willingly. He went to the cross to take the punishment of all sin of all mankind so that all who believe will have eternal life with Him.

Victor asked him if he could pray with him and he said, "Yes." Victor had him repeat the sinner's prayer and he did up until the point of saying, "In Jesus Name." The interpreter told Victor, "He doesn't want to say, 'In Jesus Name'." Victor said, "Okay." He then told him, "My hope would be that when you are at that place where you have no more hope and you are not sure of where you will be for eternity, that you would remember what I told you about the claims of who Jesus is and that you would put your hope in Him."

Victor then started asking him about his life. He asked him about his family and upbringing. This Commander told Victor that he had only a 5th grade education. He shared that he was married with 4 girls all under 10, which were not that far away. He told him his brother joined ISIS and then he was compelled to join. Victor asked him if he could pray for his wife and 4 daughters. He said, "Yes." Victor prayed that his wife and daughters would be protected, that his girls would not become hard, that his wife would have hope for a future. He prayed that they all would understand how much God Almighty loves them.

Victor then asked him, "What would you say to a young man who wanted to join ISIS?" He answered, "Don't, don't do it, get an education." He said he regretted getting involved in extremism and walking in darkness. Victor said, "Would you tell them to not go towards darkness?" He said, "Yes." Victor then asked, "Have you ever met an American?" He said "No." Then Victor asked him, "Why do you hate me and want to kill me?" He said, "I don't hate you and I don't want to kill you." He said he was shocked that Victor would offer him water and speak so gently with him. He also was very sober-minded knowing his wife and children would be living in the IDP camps.

Despite the evil this man had done, God still loves him and would forgive him and wants him in eternity with Him. Victor left with his security guy and prayed that something got through to him.

Victor's Journal Notes and Facebook Posts...

5/4/17 First, one of our team guys got shot: Please urgent prayers one of my guys Shaheen, just hours ago got shot in the stomach while trying to help rescue and get people away from ISIS. Our Humvee driver went to help downed Shaheen and he got shot as well by sniper fire from ISIS. He is also in critical condition. A little girl was also shot in the face but the FBR team has her and got her to hospital. I am in real time constant coms and they need prayer; our Humvee can't be used, it's shot to crap. Please pray for the many casualties and team with Dave & FBR, Shaheen and Muhammad. This young man is very special to me, to us, as a translator, fighter, that I recruited back in 2015 as he himself was living in an IDP camp as a scared, traumatized young man but has grown to be a heroic warrior. Please pray. Pray for the teams out there now. Tomorrow I will update Victormarx.com

"Let us then approach God's throne of grace with confidence, so that we may receive mercy and find grace to help us in our time of need." -- Hebrews 4:16

5/5/17 I hope this speaks to your heart and soul as it did mine after learning of many hurt in the last 24 hours like the little princess who was shot in the face while running away from ISIS as Iraqi army, FBR teams were fighting, rescuing, setting free over one thousand in west Mosul. (Last report she has survived.)

Please pray for the injured including of one of our team guys, Shaheen and some 20 casualties.

Shaheen is a young man that's been with us since I met and recruited him in 2015. Also, our Humvee driver was shot rescuing Shaheen. Shaheen is in critical condition in an Iraq hospital right now.

#DailyDevotional "In the book of Ezekiel, God presents the four faces of the man of God. These are the four characteristics of those who serve the Lord:

"The first is the face of a lion. The righteous are as bold as a lion, the Bible says in Proverbs 28:1. If you're not bold, then you're not righteous.

"The second face is that of an eagle. Those who wait upon the Lord "shall renew their strength; they shall mount up with wings as eagles" Isaiah 40:31 and sail into the very presence of the living God.

"The third face is the face of a man, because you will always be a human being, no matter how spiritual you think you are.

"The fourth face is that of an ox, which brings me to the point. An ox is a persistent plodder. When you feed an ox, it does not bray like a donkey. It just gets out and plows. Give it some oats and it will plow, plow, plow. More oats; more plow. No bellyaching, it just plods and plows.

"Let me tell you something, friend. God is not looking for flash and dash. He's looking for persistent plodders. Those with flash and dash will fall in the ditch. God is looking for the oxen who will put their shoulders to the wheel and pull, who are committed to discipline, determined to finish the race. God is looking for men and women who will be divine, persistent plodders to pursue the purposes of God......"
- John Hagee Ministries

5/6/17 Shaheen Update: He is going to make it!! Prayers work! Thank you everyone! This is our brave warrior who was shot a couple times in his stomach during rescue assisting getting a little girl away from ISIS. He was with FBR Team and Iraqi fighting ISIS.

He is our first team person and Yazidi young man I recruited from an IDP camp to be our Team/case worker/among other duties along with Team FBR who trained and equipped him for some of the most intense battles against ISIS. He is the first person since we went operational in 2015 to get shot after many missions and High Risk Ops.

This just sent to me from my head of security in Iraq:

"Shaheen is giving you his thumbs up after he heard my guy telling him that (Victor Marx is saying Hi.) He is in a good condition, and the emergency intensive care division they take the BULLETS out of him, he is in a stable situation right now, if you want to talk to him my guy's going to be there for the next few hours to make sure everything is OK with him, and I'm sending you a special private cell number in case you want to talk to him. If there is anything else you want please let me know. - Ali, Victor Marx Ministries, International Head of Security.

Thanks to all who offered a prayer for Shaheen and also for Muhammad who we believe is doing well. His injuries weren't as extensive as Shaheen's. We will provide all medical costs, recovery, and special housing for Shaheen for the next several months and will welcome him in our residence in Iraq for his recovery period. Thanks for continued prayer and support.

PS We will be awarding him a medal and commendation for his heroic action as well as Muhammad the Humvee driver.

Keep praying for Dave Eubank and Team FBR still out in the fight in west Mosul and us as we prepare our largest longest outreach Mission in the region. Feel free to leave Shaheen greetings on this post; he will read it in the near future and it will encourage his heart.

5/7/17 "Help these kids live," voice of Dave Eubank.
Some ministries need a church bus or van, we currently need up-armored transportation so people don't die. This is the harsh reality of what we are involved in. The armored vehicle here has been hit by ISIS in the location rescue in west Mosul. It can no longer be used and after the firefight was dragged out of the hot zone by another vehicle and chain. Here is the little girl who was shot in the face and her dad was also hurt.

All safe now but need prayers for healing! Immediate need now: Getting a new up-armored vehicle! Please pray and share because God knows what the forward Team of FBR needs next. Muhammad, our Humvee driver was shot 6x and has lived; Shaheen recovering after 2 surgeries. Also need prayer for the innocent children who have been shot and parents killed by ISIS. Our team is out there among great evil and this affects us all. Until all hear Jesus is a loving Savior!

5/14/17 Shaheen had passed away today. I can't write much through burning tears and hurting heart to those who knew and loved this amazing young man. I adopted him as my Yazidi son in my heart and life; he knew the connection we had and I gave him my word I would get him out of Iraq and eventually to the USA.

I recently offered him the first step of the journey to get him out of Iraq … he turned it down knowing his work wasn't done yet. I told him how proud of him I was and the growth and transformation into a man and warrior of valor for children. Fitting he gave his life helping a young girl. Meeting him in an IDP camp, only six months after ISIS attacked and would change him and his Yazidi people's lives forever, I saw such a hidden warriors heart beaten down by the harsh realities of ISIS having invaded his hometown of Sinjar.

In the midst of thousands in this IDP camp he made his way through the crowds surrounding me and with rough broken English told me he knew I had come to help Yazidi girls and children who had been most affected by being kidnapped by Daesh (ISIS.) We slipped out to another part of the tent city and he brought me to a 14yr old girl who had been held captive.

I saw his heart and courage to help others despite his own suffering. That is when I told him he would help me and be on Team ATP. He was excited to have a mission and since then he quietly, often without any others knowing, worked on very confidential cases to help see girls and children and families freed and then repeatedly put himself in harm's way with Team FBR on the front lines as the best most faithful Terp interpreter) we and FBR had.

I'm pouring though the many emails we exchanged and photos and videos and I'm not going to lie, I'm sad and mad at his loss.

He lived more life with courage facing his fears and destroying his once early self-assessment that he was a "coward."

If we look at actions over words, many Christian leaders I know would never dare consider themselves "a coward" and yet their actions prove otherwise as they lead many who, by the same token, live in a bubble of Bible knowledge and great westernized faith with no honorable actions of sacrifice, suffering or truly helping those like Shaheen who lived his faith!

One of the last photos was that of him holding a wounded Iraqi soldier and then soon after he would be fatally wounded, being shot in the stomach under fire by ISIS as he risked everything to move a little 10 year old girl to a safer vehicle that could drive her and her dad to safety and for further medical help after she was shot in the face by ISIS.

I am touched to have received two emails from him just before he unexpectedly passed today and I'm thankful I knew he knew without a doubt he had put his faith in Jesus Christ for eternal life as a couple years ago he told me, "Please don't forget me to bring me the Gospel."

I loved that young poet warrior who was one of the most courageous men I have been honored to know.

Evil men will pay the price for this. We will continue to help and heal the hearts of thousands as we remember the personal sacrifice of Shaheen and his selfless, courageous role in these efforts.

See you in heaven Shaheen,

Victor Marx
reachchildren.com
victorMarx.com

5/18/17 Very hard day! Fluctuating between intense anger and great sadness. Thankful for prayers for all concerned. Going through past emails from Shaheen. This from last June of Father's Day: "Happy father day for you as a father - currently you have more kids all kids you're helping them are you kids. The little kid you posted her picture with you - her mother fled from ISIS captivity recently and thanks because you're taking care to my people who are displaced. We Yazidis will remember you and love you forever; I'm pretty sure you're a good dad for your kids that's why you helping other kids especially Yazidis kids and also kids in whole the world. Thanks and have a nice time." -Regards Shaheen

I hate the pain of death, the stupidity of men and the wickedness of ISIS, Victor.
reachchildren.com
victormarx.com

5/18/17 Jesus said, "I've told you these things for a purpose: that My joy might be your joy, and your joy wholly mature. This is My command: Love one another the way I loved you. This is the very best way to love. Put your life on the line for your friends. You are My friends when you do the things I command you. I'm no longer calling you servants because servants don't understand what their master is thinking and planning. No, I've named you friends because I've let you in on everything I've heard from the Father." John 15:13-15

5/20/17 i niha dizanim êşa dilê qurûş kesek i hez kir ji bo kuştina çeteyên. Canê min her û her ji bo hemû yazidi min Nasik e, kurds, iraq, Tirk û Sûrî ku dizanin ev êş û derdê wî. ez bîra te dikim Shaheen di heman demê de dê we li ezmanan dibînin ku Îsa ji we hez dike û niha bi xatirê te rûyê wî

أنا عـارف آلآن آلآم القلب من فقدان شخص أحب أن قتيل .شيد لتق أن جميع من الأبد الى قريبة روحي. تركوس والسوريين الذين يعرفون هذا الألم والمعانة. اشتقت الى اليزيدي، كردس، العراق، اشتقت لك شاهين ولكن سوف نكركم في السما شيد يسوع يحبكم والآن ترى له وجه لوجه

'ana 'aerif alan alam alqalb min fiqdan shakhs 'ahibb 'an qutil dish. rruhi qaribatan 'iilaa al'abad min jmye alyazidi, kurds, aleiraq, twrkus walssuriiyn alladhin yaerifun hdha al'alm walmaeanatu. ashtaqat lak shahin walikan sawf nurakum fi alssama' yawed yuhibbuk walan taraa lah wajhaan liwajh

Şimdi, psilocin öldürülmesini sevdiğim birini kaybetmenin kalp ağrısını bilirim. Bu acıyı ve ıstırabını bilen benim yazıtım, kürtler, irak, türkler ve Süryanilere ruhum sonsuza kadar yakın.

This is what my heart and faith believes,

Victor Marx
reachchildren.com
PS To those who speak English don't rely on the Facebook translations it's very inaccurate.

5/23/17 As a person who has lost a very close friend and teammate in our work in Iraq who died a little over a week ago, as well as having been shot at by ISIS fighters on several occasions, and having had mortar rounds drop on us, and seen up close and personal ISIS fighters both captured and alive and the evil that is unmistakable in some and then, of course, the harsh reality of choices they made that resulted in their death, let me say, a friend of mine in the UK has very good words for Christians here in the SA: "The UK appreciates your prayers Victor Marx. FYI...to those in the USA that say, "ban the Muslims!"...let me say this... In Britain, we endured years of terror attacks from the IRA (Irish Republican Army) through the 70s and 80s in particular. It didn't make us hate all Irish Catholics. The majority of people in the UK will not let a minority of hate-filled murderers /extremists...define how we respond to our neighbours and colleagues of the Muslim faith/Hindu/Sikh or none. We will be vigilant of course...but if we let the evil minority paralyze us with fear and stop us going about our daily lives, then they have truly won. The likes of ISIS WANT the countries they attack to turn on the resident Muslims... of course they do! That way they continue to stir up more hate/fear and discord. As Christians we need to remember that GOD is in control of all things. None of this is news to Him. He allows the nations and peoples to rise and fall. We are called to tell all peoples the Gospel truth and to keep on keeping on. Victor Marx, you know me well enough to know that I don't mean this post to be disrespectful to anyone...but you also know through the work you, Eileen and the team do, that we cannot allow the evil that some men do, stop us loving our brothers and sisters from other faiths that are suffering... not "as much as" but far more than we can imagine... and who are living this nightmare every single day. xxx -- Rose"

Help us stop the next wave of youth from becoming influenced by this Dark Extremist Ideology.

Victor Marx
reachchildren.com
victormarx.com

7/26/17 Here is the Hero no one is talking about, but should be!

Thank you everyone for praying for Muhammad our friend and former Humvee driver for me and others in intense battles to liberate villages in Iraq.

He was shot 8 times when he left the damaged Humvee with a wounded girl in it who has been shot through the eye socket and ran back to the front line to get another vehicle. When he came back, Shaheen was getting out to transport the girl into the new vehicle and he was shot and Muhammad got out of the vehicle again to rescue Shaheen which he did single-handed and was shot all those times, but still got into the driver's seat after loading Shaheen into that Humvee and drove him back to the front line for medical help.

I was told when he pulled up to the friendly Iraqi forces - his unit 9th div 36th brigade - he opened his door and fell out, riddled with bullet holes. He miraculously survived and we spent some time visiting. He even helped us deliver lion and lamb healing toys last week to children. But he went in for a final surgery remove a sniper's round from his neck. He is out of surgery and says thank you to all Team ATP for prayers! He's a family man and is growing in his faith! I love this brother and even though Shaheen died 10 days later, Muhammad was one of the few people there for Shaheen even though he has been shot so many times. He visited Shaheen and shared some final words given for me to know. Sobering they are as Shaheen wanted me to keep reaching children that's why he became part of what we were doing.

What's holding you back from doing great things for the glory of God!!?? Happy for Muhammad and yet still grieving for Shaheen,

Victor Marx
reachchildren.com
victormarx.com

7/29/17 Special Prayer if you could offer a quick one. I'm sitting in my hotel room with my faithful K-9 Scout in Ocean City, New Jersey preparing to address several hundred men tonight, who need (and many want) to hear from God and do great things with Him. Yet, I found a video clip I haven't seen since it was recorded out west of Mosul, Iraq where we trying to move the needle a little helping children and families who were being held by ISIS in villages. Shaheen, the Yazidi warrior poet and hero of children seen in the video was one of the closest young men to my heart. I recruited him to work with us and with FBR. He later was killed and is a true martyr for the faith, enduring absolutely the worst of conditions trying to help save a girl and her father. The girl was shot through eye socket and lived, Shaheen didn't.

The driver of our Humvee is Muhammad that I've posted much about lately, was shot 8 times by ISIS snipers on the same mission and yet he was able to save Shaheen who was down. He pulled him into the new Humvee (with NO cover fire!) with 8 rounds in him - one in the neck - by ISIS snipers. He managed to drive Shaheen to the back line and then when he opened the door, he fell out and yet amazing he lived. Shaheen lived 10 days then succumbed.

I was just with Muhammad last week in Iraq. We shed some tears missing our friend and fellow warrior.

So, all that to say, I sit here in this room feeling so many emotions from anger mixed with hot tears, trying to process my last two months, holding babies whose parents were shot to death by ISIS in Mosul; remembering a huge mortar round that hit so close to us that shrapnel peppered the wall in a street where we were in deep Mosul. It was within feet of us; the angle saved us and I must think our guardian angels as well were with us.

The responsibility is so heavy to have the privilege to address these men tonight at the STANDING STRONG Men's Gathering. I'm honored and humbled and really ask for your prayers that God's Spirit would give me exactly what I need to say and have His felt presence there to break down walls of lies in men's hearts so that He can build spiritual warriors up for aggressive advancement against the forces of darkness and build His Kingdom, because ISIS is NOT the ultimate evil, they are only manifestations of the wicked one.

We live in Evil days and we men must stand Courageously, be Bold, be Strong in the Lord and Brave to do what needs to be done starting in our lives, our homes, our work, our neighborhoods, our churches, our states, our country and our world.

Thanks for taking a moment to just offer a little prayer to the Lord on our behalf. I am very thankful for you to do that.

Victor Marx

chapter forty three

My Tribute to
My Adopted Son, Shaheen

This final chapter is dedicated to Shaheen, A True Warrior!

Shaheen succumbed to his wounds. He was an amazing young man who I adopted as my Yazidi son in my heart and life. I recently offered him the first step of the journey to get him out of Iraq ... he turned it down knowing his work wasn't done yet. I told him how proud of him I was seeing the transformation and growth into a man of God and warrior of valor for children. It is so fitting that he gave his life helping a young girl escape to freedom.

Meeting him in an IDP camp only six months after ISIS attacked and would change him and his Yazidi people's lives forever, I saw such a hidden warrior's heart beaten down by the harsh realities of ISIS having invaded his town of Sinjar.

In the midst of thousands in this IDP camp he made his way through the crowds surrounding me and with rough broken English knew I had come to help the Yazidi girls and children who had most been affected by being kidnapped by Daesh (ISIS). We slipped out to another part of the tent city and he brought me to a 14 year old girl who had been captive.

I saw his heart and courage to help others despite his own suffering. That is when I told him he would help me and be on Team ATP. He was excited to have a mission and since then he quietly, often without any others knowing, worked on very confidential cases to help see girls and children and their families freed and then repeatedly put himself in harm's way with Team FBR on the front lines as the best most faithful interpreter our teams ever had.

He lived his life with courage, facing his fears, and destroying his once early self-assessment that he was a "coward."

One of the last photos I have was that of him holding a wounded Iraqi soldier. Soon after that he, himself, would be fatally wounded, being shot in the stomach under fire by ISIS as he risked everything to help a little 10 year old girl. They were moving her to a safer vehicle that could drive her and her dad to safety and for further medical help after she was shot in the face by ISIS.

I am touched to have received two emails from him just before he unexpectedly passed away and I'm thankful to know that he knew, without a doubt, he had put his faith in Jesus Christ for eternal life. A couple of years ago he told me, "Please don't forget me to bring me the Gospel!"

I loved that young poet warrior who was one of the most courageous men I have been honored to know.

Evil men will pay the price. We will continue to honor his courage as we continue to help and heal the hearts of the thousands that he loved and served.

See you in heaven Shaheen!

chapter forty four

"Triggered" the Movie

With this 3rd revised edition of The Victor Marx Story, we are happy to announce the availability of our new film *Triggered - Military Edition* and *Triggered Too* (Civilian Edition).

These documentary films highlight the personal struggles of military personnel, first responders, civilians, and their families with the realities of trauma recovery and healing.

NO ONE IS IMMUNE FROM TRAUMA!

Nearly everyone will experience some form of trauma. Accidents, mental or physical abuse, violence, injury, illness, or the death of a loved one can cause post-traumatic stress (PTS). If the PTS is serious and not resolved, it can become post-traumatic stress disorder (PTS(d) and its victims may suffer devastating effects.

PTS(d) does not discriminate. It can take down the strong and the weak, change behavior, cause addictions, destroy marriages and families, and even take the lives of its victims. As many as 22 veterans per day take their own lives due to PTS(d).

In Triggered, renowned trauma expert Victor Marx, himself a victim of PTS(d), takes the viewer on a journey to understand PTS(d), its symptoms and treatments, and to find hope for recovery. Unscripted, raw and authentic interviews with PTS(d) victims and insightful interviews with experts in the field, reveal how victims can free themselves from its life-crippling effects, and offers encouragement and hope for not only those who suffer from PTS(d) but also for those who love them.

For more information and helpful resources or to order your own copy of the films on DVD please visit our online store at: victormarx.com or watch free on Victor's YouTube Channel.

Epilogue

FILMING THE VICTOR MARX STORY

The decision to put my life story on film was made so I could "virtually" visit every youth facility in the nation with my message of hope and transformation through a personal relationship with Jesus Christ. The filming became a journey in itself with much spiritual warfare and many miracles to bring the project to completion.

As we were getting ready to travel to Memphis, Tennessee in October of 2011 to film the opening and reenactment scenes, we asked for prayer in our weekly e-newsletter as we were preparing our trip for the next week. That very same day, we received an email from Canice McGovern telling us they had watched an interview on TV (one of four we had done earlier in the year) at a friend's house just that past Saturday where they were celebrating her friend, Sunne Davis' 60th birthday. Sunne said she wanted them all to "watch a taped interview she had where the man had this amazing testimony that took place in the house that her mother had bought years ago." She said her mother "bought the house that Victor had lived in; the one that he spoke about in the TV interview, where God had supernaturally protected Victor and his family from his step-father's wrath..." Canice went on to say, "As I watched this interview, I had an anxiety attack, recalling memories from my childhood... I look forward to reading his book and to experiencing the healing that takes place at the hands of a loving Father..."

Eileen emailed Canice and also inquired as to how to contact her friend and her friend's mother. After receiving the information, my assistant Trudy made contact with her friend and spoke with her and her mother, Mrs. Lillie Barron. Ms. Lillie, a true Southern Lady, invited us to interview her at her home. She also told us that her neighbor, Mrs. Betty Carlisle still remembers the night it all happened – when we escaped out the window of what is now Ms. Lillie's home and ran to Ms. Betty's home for shelter. Ms. Lillie told my assistant that she felt somehow like I was a close relation to her and that Ms. Betty was very excited to be able to see me after all these years and asked after my mother and the other children. (Ms. Lillie is the lady I had met approximately ten years before when I first found the house again and where she told me she had found our family photos and had been praying for us all those years!) So, plans were made for me and the film crew to make the drive from Memphis down to Hattiesburg to interview Ms. Lillie and Ms. Betty.

Now, as I was looking at the map of the road from Memphis to Hatties-burg, I saw that Mendenhall was right on the way...Mendenhall being the locale of the chicken houses and that commercial cooler the child molester locked me in to leave me for dead and also the locale of my Mammaw's house and the hanging tree. Man, this was no coincidence... it was the Lord mapping this all the way! The interviews with Ms. Lillie and Ms. Betty at the house we had escaped from; the scenes at the site of the cooler; the hanging tree; and porch at Mammaw's house... It truly was affirmation from our loving Lord that His hand was on this film from start to finish! And, as we were to discover, His intended use of the film has gone far and beyond what we had originally planned or could even have imagined as we see lives being touched by its message all over the world. Now available in fifteen languages the film has even greater po-tential to reach hurting youth and adults.

I am truly humbled and grateful at what the Lord has done with my life story and thank Him for His daily grace and mercy toward me and mine. PS: Canice was to share later: "I am reminded of the day when I sat on Sunne's couch, watching an interview on Sky Angel, where Victor shared the heart-wrenching story of his childhood...I was molested as a child, so hearing Victor's story had a traumatic effect on me as I sat there watching and listening. Apparently, no one sitting around me noticed what I was going through, because my husband and children's eyes were glued to the TV screen. That night, as I lay in bed, remembering what I had seen and experienced, I felt the overwhelming "need" to order Victor's book, and share copies with some people I knew who also faced sexual abuse as children. The next day I called Sunne to get Victor's name and then found him online. I am happy to hear that this led to Victor finding Sunne's mom, Ms. Lillie, and the neighbor, Ms. Betty. I can see where God works in and through ALL THINGS for our good and HIS glory. Praise His name!"

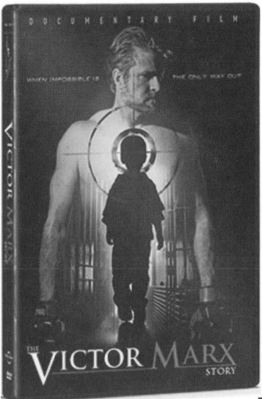

DVD in 15 subtitles including *English

Audio Book on 3 CDs

*English subtitles for the Hearing impaired

The Victor Marx Story on DVD and Audio Book available in the All Things Possible Store at: www.victormarx.com

AUTHOR BIOGRAPHY

Victor Marx is the founding director of All Things Possible Ministries, dedicated to reaching at-risk and incarcerated youth. He holds a Seventh Degree Keichu-Do Karate Black Belt, a Seventh Degree in Jiu-Jitsu, and a Fourth Degree in weapons. He has trained law enforcement officers and special military forces. He and his wife Eileen and their five children live in southern California.

All Things Possible Ministries
P.O. Box 63176
Colorado Springs, CO 80962
www.victormarx.com

ABOUT THE CO-AUTHORS

Wayne Atcheson is the author of six books including Impact for Christ, the 40-year history of the Fellowship of Christian Athletes. Wayne has served on the national staff of the FCA, as Sports Information Director at the University of Alabama, and on the Jerry B. Jenkins Christian Writers Guild staff in Colorado Springs. In 2006 he was named Director of the Billy Graham Library in Charlotte, NC.

James Werning is a freelance author, radio producer, and founder of Peacedude Productions (www.peacedude.net).

WHAT OTHERS ARE SAYING

"When Victor shares his story, people of all ages respond to Jesus Christ. Many young people and adults easily relate to Victor's openness in sharing his story."
—Wayne Atcheson, Director Billy Graham Library

"Victor Marx is one of the top martial artists in the country. I have never seen anybody with faster hands than Victor! It's almost beyond your ability to see what he is doing when he goes into action! (He) has written one of the most fascinating books I have ever read about how God can take a broken life and redeem it for His purposes. You will cry, laugh and rejoice as you read it... Thank God for Victor and his ministry."
—LT General (Ret.) William G. Boykin; Former Commander of U. S. Army Special Forces; Founding Member of Delta Force; Kingdom Warriors Ministry

"Victor lived through experiences that both toughened and matured him. You would expect him to be a little on the mean side. However, Victor has a tender heart. He knows what it is like to bear the scars of life's unpleasant surprises and he is committed to helping others prepare for those challenges. I wholeheartedly recommend that you engage Victor Marx."
—Gary Walsh, LT Colonel (Ret.) U. S. Army

"I know I have faced my share of adversity. After 14 years in the SEAL teams and many deployments downrange to both Afghanistan and Iraq, one thing I know for sure is that sometimes life can be tough. When you choose such a life you expect adversity and if you're not ready for it you're not preparing the way you should. I recently met Victor Marx and he shared his story of the trials and adversity he faced starting at age 5 and continuing throughout his

childhood. I still can't put into words the many different emotions I have felt trying to comprehend what he must have gone through. The terror, the pain, the hopelessness: how does a child prepare for that? There is no schooling, no instruction that can prepare us for such things at such a young age. Yet despite everything he endured he continued to press forward, to fight, and to persevere. I am a better man for knowing him and I am thankful to count Victor Marx a friend and a brother."
—Senior Chief David A. Hansen, Navy SEAL, Sailor of the Year – 2007

"Victor Marx is a breed of warrior that can inspire all of us to action. I saw Victor at an event at my church where the presence of the Holy Spirit was so strong, that every word spoken was deep, hard-hitting, and just what men of faith need to hear. Fathers, husbands, and sons have been banding together like the brothers we are to fight the evil that continues to grow in our world. Men of character, love, compassion, and courage are called to serve our King, and ATP Ministries is showing us how it's done. Men and women in prison need to hear the Good News that they are forgiven and become new creatures in Him. Victor's courage to do this is extremely inspirational to me, calling me to action too."
—Randy Kelley, Former Navy SEAL Sniper and Entrepreneur

"You have shown me what Christianity looks like by the way you love people. I would like Victor's book in Arabic to be able to give to the soldiers and Iraq government leaders."
—General Mustafa, Iraqi Army

"Growing up in Los Angeles, CA, seconds away from where the 1992 LA riots started, I needed ways to stay out of trouble. With few after-school programs and lots of free time, I often found myself exposed to the negative aspects of the inner city. Victor Marx has truly been a blessing to the community and to me. He has helped me to improve and become a better son, father, husband, and man."
—Kevin Burnett, NFL Linebacker

"Victor Marx is a true human being. His honesty and forthrightness are unquestionable. His belief and passion for our youth is honorable. I believe in Victor Marx and his mission. I hope that you will be touched by his commitment like I have."
—Frank Shamrock, 5X UFC Undefeated Champion and Actor

"It was great meeting the other day. I started your book. Wow, what a story! I can honestly say I was inspired by what you went through."
—Bill Romanowski, NFL Linebacker; 4 Super Bowl Championships

"The interview with Victor Marx on our Life, Love and Family radio program was one of the most powerful stories and interviews we have ever done. What an amazing story of redemption and forgiveness; of healing and hope that he found in a personal relationship with Jesus Christ. His All Things Possible Ministries to help youth and others find the same hope and overcome abuse, abandonment, PTSD, etc. is to be commended. Truly God never wastes a wound..."
—Dr. Tim Clinton, President - American Association of Christian Counselors

"I met Victor and Eileen at the recording of Life Today with James Robison. I had an instant connection with Victor. His powerful and emotional story is inspiring and evidence of God's grace. Victor has done the difficult part by making the changes necessary to live a healthy and productive life! Victor has real-world credibility that he uses for God's glory."
—Charles S. Lowery, Ph.D. President, Lowery Institute for Excellence - Speaker, Author

"The greatest thing that could happen to a tough guy like Victor Marx is that he was defeated by God's love. Amazing."
—Nicky Cruz, President and Founder of Nicky Cruz Outreach & TRUCE

"What's amazing is that Victor survived his childhood and what is even more amazing is that the Lord is using him now to reach so many hurting youth."
—Dr. James Dobson, Founder - Focus on the Family; Host - Family Talk Radio

"Victor Marx is impossible to sum up. He's my kind of crazy. He's Jesus crazy and that's the only kind of crazy that matters."
—Eric Metaxas, NY Times Best-selling Author, Speaker, and Radio Host

"I have known Victor for a number of years and his heart for those who find themselves in apparent hopelessness has not changed. His testimony and work through All Things Possible continues to bring light and hope into the darkness of those in captivity."
—Del Tackett, Architect and Teacher of The Truth Project ; Senior Correspondent and Co-Host for CrossExamine.com

"Victor Marx is a warrior for Christ and one of the strongest and most courageous men of God that I know. He exemplifies leadership in ways that defy words and his contribution to be one of our foremost speakers at our Kingdom Men's Gatherings has been nothing short of incredible."
—Frank Sontag, President, Kingdom Men's Gathering and Radio Host

"Victor is a valiant Warrior for Christ who simply commands attention without saying a word. Talk about "street cred!" What he can do for the kids in The System is so unique and critical. I like to think of Victor as our own little version of Michael the Archangel. God Bless Victor Marx!"
—Frank Pastore, The Frank Pastore Show - 99.5 FM KKLA Los Angeles

"A.T.P. Ministries is there for those lost, that few have hope for, and where fewer are willing to go."
—Gary Heavin, Founder of Curves Int'l

"Victor, we owe you a debt of gratitude for the outstanding work you are doing."
—Drayton McLane, Owner of Houston Astros

"His mesmerizing, caring, and genuine personality has troubled youth falling in line to give their life to Christ. It's simply miraculous! This is why we support him."
—Paul J. Meyer, Founder of Success Motivation International Inc., 40+ companies; New York Times best-selling author

"As a former Air Force A-10 fighter pilot and Super Bowl Champion with the Dallas Cowboys, I appreciate toughness, grit, perseverance, and being a leader of men. Victor not only exemplifies those traits, but he exemplifies the greatest trait a man can personify -- he is a humble man who loves the Lord. He has utilized all the pain early in his life for God's greater good. He is a man who lives by God's promise that "All things work for the good for those who love Him and are called according to His purpose." I highly recommend Victor as a husband, as a father, as a friend, and as a mighty man of God."
—Chad Hennings, A-10 pilot, 45 missions in Northern Iraq in Operation Provide Comfort; 3 X Super Bowl Champion with the Dallas Cowboys; Founder Wingmen Ministries

"Leadership can be described in a multitude of ways, with endless claims and scenarios to back these definitions. But most people will agree that a truly great leader - a leader that places the well-being of others above

his own self - will have these few traits embedded in the bedrock of their character – HONOR – VALUES – INTEGRITY. Victor Marx is one of these leaders. I have had the privilege of sharing my thoughts and teachings with Victor. Coming from a Marine infantry background with multiple combat deployments, and currently working as an agent with the United States #1 executive protection firm, I have seen the consequences of terrible leadership and training. I have never seen a more professional instructor and mentor in my life! The way Victor communicates his skill set to his students will make you a believer!"
—Andrew Farlaino, USMC Infantry/Combat Instructor; Agent - Gavin De Becker & Associates

"When you talk with Victor Marx you immediately sense the love of Jesus in him and his genuine kindness towards others. But please don't mistake Victor's kindness for weakness because he is one serious "Cajun" warrior. Victor is a world class martial artist and champion who uses his talents as well as his own personal adversities to share the love of Christ and the message of forgiveness with troubled youth. For the past many years, Victor has led hundreds of incarcerated kids to the Lord. Victor is a Godly man with a humble spirit, who serves the Lord. Murrieta is truly blessed to have his ATP Cajun Karate Training Academy and "All Things Possible" Ministry as part of the community. I am honored to call Victor Marx my friend."
—Mike Baray, Chief of Police (Ret.) – Murrieta California Police Dept.

"Victor Marx and his ministry provide living testament that with faith in God, all things are indeed possible. Victor is not only a master of martial arts and the dynamics of physical power; he is a master of the spiritual power of the word of God. He has the unparalleled ability to teach troubled youth to open their hearts to the blessings of life through their own spiritual awakening. Victor reaches them by revealing his own incredible experiences in life in his unique and powerful blend of personal wisdom and humor, which showcase the true majesty of life and the infinite power of finding your redemption in the Lord. Victor is living proof that there is hope for all who seek it, truth for all who believe it, and salvation for all who choose it."

Pastors and Ministry Leaders:

"Pastors, I want to encourage you to come and see the newly released film, ": When Impossible is the Only Way Out". We just showed it at our church and literally had a line of people wrapped around our campus waiting to get in.

It's difficult to live a hellish story, but retelling it is even more difficult and a very emotional undertaking. Only God can bring such beauty out of abuse, triumph out of tragedy, and such fragrance from a trodden rose petal. Come see how Victor's story of unfolds."
—Brian Bell, Sr. Pastor - Calvary Chapel Murrieta, California

"I've known Victor and his family personally for many years. They're the real deal! We've done outreaches with them in our church numerous times and the result has always been the same – Changed lives! Their work in the prisons with young incarcerated youth is also essential as they seek to reach a group of kids often forgotten. Thank you, Victor, for your work!"
—Ron Hindt, Sr. Pastor - Calvary Houston, Texas

"I'm not sure if a true-life story can be more honest and relate better to hurting people than Victor's story. He presents a kaleidoscope of deep emotional pain, joy, disappointment and hope which flashes across the pages of 'The Victor Marx story: With God Are Possible.' If you have ever suffered in life, young or old, God can bring hope and healing through this book!"
—Bill Stonebraker, Author & Senior Pastor – Calvary Chapel Honolulu

"I have known Victor Marx a long time. His passion for Jesus Christ is genuine and strong, and God is using him to touch many lives. Victor is a great model of what God can do in and through a life dedicated to His glory. I commend his ministry to you."
—Greg Laurie, Pastor/Evangelist - Harvest Christian Fellowship and Harvest Crusades

"Victor Marx is on 'the cutting edge'! He's a Sharp Servant that will cut quickly to the Heart of Life, deep into the real issues of day to day living. Victor's open and forthright approach affords him a listening audience with some of the most challenging groups of people in need of The Lord's Touch. These are folks that others avoid. But not Victor Marx. He's on a Mission and God has His hand upon him."
—Dr. Dennis "The Swan" Swanberg, Author & Speaker - Swanberg Ministries

"I have known Victor for over 10 years and have watched with great joy as God has raised him up to be a light in darkness, a wounded warrior who is changing the lives of thousands. He has spoken numerous times at The Road and has been used of God to set so many captives free. Our world needs true

life, authentic, robust men of God who have been shackled by Satan and set free. Victor does just that. With humor, realism, and power, God is using Victor's story—both live and in his new movie—to bring hope and healing to thousands. I highly recommend Victor and his movie."
—Dr. Steve Holt, Senior Pastor, The Road @ Chapel Hills, Colorado Springs

"In Victor and Eileen Marx I have observed firsthand the fruit of both the character of Christ in their lives and the evangelistic fruit in their ministry. They have a true gift of evangelism, matched with a passionate fire to reach out to youth that have been marginalized by drugs, gangs, or by being born into adverse circumstances. As with Jesus, they have been anointed to preach good news to the poor, to bind up the broken-hearted, the recovering of sight to the blind, and the setting of prisoners free. (Luke 4:18)"
—Danny Lehmann, Evangelism Representative – Youth With A Mission International Honolulu, Hawaii

"We live in an age where we would be shocked to learn of the number of individuals who have experienced violent or sexual abuse who silently suffer the residual pains in our congregations. The Victor Mark Story is, I believe, a must-see for our generation. The movie instills hope for those greatly wounded by traumatic life events, while the power of forgiveness is clearly revealed. This true and touching story of one man's journey to find the healing and hope that can only come from God is a great tool to help others find hope and healing both in and outside of the church! I highly recommend it!"
—Barry Stagner, Sr. Pastor - Calvary Chapel Tustin, California

"I have had the blessing of knowing Victor Marx for over twenty years, and I never cease to be amazed at how God uses him in so many different ways to reach out to so many people across all walks of life! His transparency and sincerity in Jesus allow him to be incredibly effective as a minister for the gospel, especially with the youth of this new generation! I am grateful for his friendship and I look forward to watching God's continued hand of blessing in his life."
—Joey Buran, Sr. Pastor - Worship Generation Fountain Valley, California

"Victor Marx speaks from his heart with passion, conviction, and the truth that Jesus' death and resurrection was the power in his life that empowered him to overcome the extreme abuse he suffered as a child at the hands of

those who should have loved and protected him. Together with his extensive skill of martial arts, self-effacing humor and sincere love for the lost, he impacts and inspires all who hear him speak. I highly recommend you invite him to your church and allow God to use him to minister to and set the captives free who have either suffered the same as he as a boy, or were even the abuser."

—Ray Bentley, Sr. Pastor - Maranatha Chapel San Diego, California

"In the last 15 years, I have been privileged to be the director here at Calvary Chapel Christian Camp, I have seen very few speakers connect and captivate the students the way Victor does with the message of hope that is the heart of the Gospel. Whether it is the tongue in cheek Cajun humor or foot to face martial arts demos, Victor is a rare combination that grabs the kids and delivers the knockout that is "Christ in you the hope of Glory" of Col. 1:27. Whether it is from the pulpit, podium, platform or playground, I could not recommend more highly the ministry that Victor has through "All Things Possible." We consider it a wonderful investment to support his ministry as our urban missionary to the locked up and lost in the juvenile correctional facilities around the U.S., as well as a valiant warrior for the souls of our kids here at camp."

—Jeff Gill, Sr. Pastor – Calvary Chapel South Bay Gardena, California

"Victor Marx is unique. Almost a perfect combination of Chuck Norris and Don Knotts. As a martial artist he is rather a "lethal clown". As a minister of the Gospel he is likewise so very effective while being incredibly entertaining. I have seen audiences cut deeply to the heart by his delivery of the Word and his testimony and seen them weep while they laugh."

—Ken Graves, Sr. Pastor - Calvary Chapel Bangor, Maine

"I highly recommend Victor and his ministry because it preaches the truth and he has a heart for the lost. Victor is a man of integrity and loves truth; this is what the Kingdom of God is all about."

—Raul Ries, Sr. Pastor - Calvary Chapel Golden Springs, California

"Victor Marx is a man that loves his wife and children – in some sense of the statement, it is unheard of in many circles in today's decaying society. This man is a friend that always remains your friend and will stand beside you during difficult times.

Victor Marx is a man of discipline –his achievements in the martial arts can

speak for themselves, and I will let them do so. He can do more damage with his right thumb than most people could with their entire bodies. Yet the discipline of love is a power beyond Victor Marx. May reading this book inspire you; may it cause any anger or hatred to dissipate from your heart as you learn the love that God has for you and for anyone you may know that has a weary soul."
—Mike MacIntosh, Sr. Pastor - Horizon Christian Fellowship San Diego, California

"Over the years, we have had Victor Marx share his wonderful ministry with our youth, as well as our annual men's conference, and I would like to say that his personal relationship with Jesus Christ is most definitely reflected in his commitment to today's youth. He has such a unique style and ease in his presentation, and we have been blessed to see many respond as he shares of God's goodness and mercy at our youth outreaches. We love him, and recommend his ministry without reservation."
—David Rosales, Sr. Pastor - Calvary Chapel Chino Valley, California

"Victor Marx has left an indelible mark in the hearts and minds of our congregation. Weeks after he taught for our Sunday services, I still heard our congregation speaking about how Victor's testimony impacted their life. It was our joy and honor to host our friend, Victor!"
—Pancho Juarez, Sr. Pastor - Calvary Chapel Montebello, California

"[Victor Marx] One of my most passionate fellow travelers on the evangelical road, whose story is remarkable... Victor told me that he and I have much in common except that my disability challenges are quite visible while his are hidden from sight, locked inside his mind and spirit... People often say they don't know how I've created such a meaningful and fulfilling life despite my lack of limbs. Yet I am blessed in more ways than I can count. I think life would be far more difficult for someone who lacks a loving family like the one I had. Sadly, Victor grew up in a broken home, and it is no wonder that he once felt broken himself."
—Nick Vujicic in his book, Unstoppable; Life Without Limbs Ministry

"We watched it [] last night with our friend who is visiting from Arkansas; very well done and very powerful, Victor! I know it was gut-wrenching stuff, but you are right - to find out God's redemptive perspective on what we go through, He sometimes takes us back through the dark passages of our lives

with the Light of Life lifted high. God is not affected by our darkness. There is not even a shadow in Him and His promise is to make all things new. Thanks for being a loud testimony to the Truth - He is the Resurrection and the Life. The works of the Adversary can be undone and those parts of us that were killed by his evil works will be rejuvenated. Flesh for the dry bone and breath for the vacuum of death. That suction is swallowing whole generations of babies and children right now. Thank you for hearing the call to go after them. One of my favorite parts is seeing Eileen and hearing her share her thoughts. I'm so glad it is a joint venture. That's perhaps an unintelligible, but subliminally loaded, message to this generation whose religion is Personal Sovereignty, the core of all satanic religion..."

—Terry and Nancy Clark – Catalyst Ministries San Clemente, California

LETTERS FROM CHILDREN

"I'm writing because I just finished your book today. You really touched my heart and made me see God's true ability for me, the love He has for me, for all of us. There is still hope for me with God."
—Banisha, Orange County Juvenile Detention Center

"I have a great desire to share with you that I have read your book called "gs Are Possible." Your book has made a great impact in my life. I can hardly find words to express how your book has changed my life. I have surrendered my life to Jesus, and I want now my spirit to be fully awakened and live my life with Jesus as I have never known it before."
—Bianca, Incarcerated, Santa Ana

"Your story was very powerful it taught me so much. Some of the things your story taught me were: *God has a plan for everybody.

*Everybody that has a painful childhood can become a survivor. *To believe that God really does help you, no matter what you have done in the past. I really liked how you took what has happened to you and looked to God for help. I liked how you put Bible verses in the book to go along with what you were describing. That's awesome!"
—Danae, Juvenile Home, Iowa

"As a staff member...I have never seen the Lord work in the students' lives as much as He did tonight. Praise God for the incredible ministry he is using you in. May He bless you, and keep you. May His Spirit go before you, with you, and after you."
—Javier, Staff Member, prison for boys

"Well I'm writing you this letter cause you and God really spoke to me. I can really relate to your story, I really loved your book. I read it about 4 times well."
—Carlos, Orange County Juvenile Detention Center

"Thank you for your good book. I really enjoyed it. I just got it and I'm already finished with it. This is the first book I have ever finish reading. Seriously, Victor, your book is great. I'm going to tell my new dad to read it. I just found out I have a real dad. He just got out of prison. He didn't know that he had a daughter."
—Jessica, Locked up teenage gang member

Hey Victor,
Thanks for the speech. It helped some of my own doors open. It was like you took my heart out and sewed it shut. I felt the Lord there while you were talking. I'm scared cause I might be going to look out for my commitment. So, I was wondering if you could pray for me. I'm sorry for what happened to you 'cause I was sexually abused too. People label me as a sex offender because of what another man taught me. How can God forgive me for the things I've done? You asked how I label Jesus and my answer to that is he is a Father that no one can amount to. You are one of a few MEN in my life. I would like to be friends with you. I think that God sent you to specifically help me and a couple others. I hope that you write back and tell your wife the same thing.
God Bless,
—Matthew [a juvenile offender]

Victor,
It's me, the life you changed. Last night, the night you came, I was in my room crying asking God to send me an Angel who would let me know I could break this cycle. I had no idea we were going to hear you speak, but when I did I was shocked, because your exact words were that 'we could break the cycle.' In that hour my life changed.

When you prayed for our burdens to be lifted, I can't explain why but it felt like a two-ton rock was lifted from me. You are my angel and for that I give you thanks. Your wife was explaining that God had a calling for me, so I prayed. Today I realized he wants me to help those who can't help themselves. I guess what I am trying to say is thank you. I hope and pray

you write me back so that I can talk more deeply with you. I only ask that you pray for me as I pray for you.
—Renae [a juvenile offender]

"Hey, Victor, it is Shawn...a person whose life you changed to a life of following Christ Jesus! You came to Iowa to help and lead others to Christ and that is what you did."
—Shawn, Former Locked Up Teen

"I really was touched after reading your story about your life background, the good, the bad and the worst that you went through until the time you came to know God. I got the book from a very good friend of mine who visited me in prison shortly after I had been convicted and as he was about to leave, left me with the novel entitled, "All Things Possible" ...and in no time read the interesting story. The amazing part of the story is that it is similar to my background, it was as if I were the one."
—Stephen, Maximum Security Prison, Zambia, Africa

appendix A

A WORD FROM EILEEN MARX, VICTOR MARX'S WIFE

You may be married to someone who has experienced childhood abuse, resulting in Post-Traumatic Stress Disorder (PTSD), and because of this your marriage has endured great challenges and difficulties.

These challenges may vary from outbursts of anger to substance abuse to physical and verbal abuse and even infidelity. All of these are so painful and very destructive on a marriage. In fact, we all know couples that haven't made it because the problems that can result from these behaviors are more than the spouse can take.

I understand the pain and emotions that are attached to some of these behaviors. A person doesn't endure childhood abuse without wounds, and if these wounds are not healed properly (acknowledged, validated, cleansed, healing oil applied personally from the Lord Jesus with His truth), these wounds just fester with infection and eventually infect the whole person, causing all kinds of collateral damage, which could result in divorce, abuse, addictions, repeating the abuse upon others or even suicide.

Fortunately, God kept my husband from these devastating consequences out of his own desperate desire to stop the cycle of alcoholism, abuse, divorce, drug addiction and infidelity he experienced in his own family growing up. It caused him to cling to the only One who could keep him from these destructive cycles, that being the Person of Jesus Christ!

Even so, our marriage got to a point where I gave Victor an ultimatum: If he did not get deep, emotional help to intervene and stop the chaos, I was going to pack up our children and move out. Let me be clear, I was never thinking "divorce" but I was demanding action for change. This was the catalyst God used to start the painful healing process within my Victor's heart, soul, and mind. We were so grateful to find a committed, God-fearing psychologist who specialized in childhood abuse. The process of emotional healing takes so much courage, vulnerability, and a desperate motivation to have freedom - true freedom!

The most important thing you can do as a spouse as they begin this process is to let them know that you will be there with them, you are not going anywhere, no matter how long it takes. This would fall under your vows: through sickness and health, good times and bad. Your spouse needs that promise of faithful commitment as an anchor when the process of healing ebbs and flows with feelings of anxiety and fear.

What if God brought you into your spouse's life to be an instrument of His love, to be His hands, heart and voice that would be a crucial part of your spouse's healing? Wouldn't it be worth all the difficulties and hardships you have endured?

I'm speaking to you from my own experiences: walking through the healing process with my husband, witnessing his heart, soul and mind being healed, watching God use his painful childhood to help thousands of hurting people start their own healing as they allow God to bring them to their own freedom. It has been worth it all!

Jesus indeed brings beauty from ashes!

Saved by Amazing Grace!

appendix B
by Dr. Arlys McDonald

IF YOU HAVE BEEN ABUSED

If you have been abused or molested, the most important thing for you to know is that God wants you to be healed. You can rise above your place of pain and desperation! People don't accidentally break a bone and say, "Well, I guess I'll have to live with this for the rest of my life." No! They go to the hospital and get treated and hopefully they are as good as new in a few months. Doctors say that bones are actually stronger at the point of fracture after they've properly healed.

It's the same with emotional wounds. I have watched so many people be healed of devastating trauma and abuse, and now they are able to help others who are hurting. Like it says in the Bible:

"You plotted evil against me, but God turned it into good so that many lives might be saved." – Genesis 50:20
So, the first step in the healing process is to *want to be healed*.

Secondly ask God to heal you and believe that He can do it! He is the God of healing and restoration and new beginnings. God's desire is ...
"... to comfort all those who grieve ... to give them crowns instead of ashes, the oil of joy instead of tears of grief, and clothes of praise instead of a spirit of weakness. They will be called Oaks of Righteousness." – Isaiah 61:2-3

Thirdly you must seek help from a Christian counselor who is experienced with cases of trauma. Or you might at least begin by speaking with your pastor or priest. Healing begins when you tell somebody about it. That's also when you'll uncover all kinds of anger and confusion and guilt and shame and emotions you maybe didn't even know you had.

But talking about it is not enough. I strongly recommend a type of therapy called EMDR for people who have been seriously abused and traumatized. This tried and true method involves dealing with lies and abuse from the past, which might sound like a scary thing – especially if you've spent years trying to forget the past. But you can never truly move forward unless you go back in your mind to the place where you were hurt. It's like having a wound that won't heal because there's a splinter inside. You can't keep ignoring it – eventually you'll need to go straight to the source of infection. But thankfully you're not alone in this process. Jesus will help you quickly come to a place of healing if you will only let Him.

"God Himself has said, 'I will not in any way fail you nor give you up nor leave you without support. I will not in any degree leave you helpless nor forsake you nor let you down!'" – Hebrews 13:5 (Amplified)

You might wonder how to find a good Christian counselor who is knowledgeable and sensitive to the issues that you are facing. The following organization has a great counselor referral network. You may call anonymously and ask for a recommendation, or search their website: The American Association of Christian Counselors, 1-800-526-8673, www.aacc.net

Finally, if you are in an abusive relationship right now, then *get out!* Don't wait another day. Get away from the abuser now! And if necessary, get help from a church, or a counselor, or a state agency, or simply dial 911 on the phone. Don't wait another hour!

You may have experienced horrible abuse at the hands of people in the past, but I want you to know that God can be trusted. Jesus loves you and He has a wonderful plan and a purpose for your life which includes healing.

"I know the plans that I have for you, declares the Lord. They are plans for peace and not disaster, plans to give you a future filled with hope." – Jeremiah 29:11

Be encouraged! You need not stay in a place of desperation anymore.

Whatever your past may be, you have a wonderful future if you will only trust God and seek the help you need.

What's more, I want you to know that I believe in you and hopefully someday you can tell me about the miraculous healing that God has done in your life. You are a very special person, created by God for a wonderful purpose. I pray that you will experience many, many blessings of healing and peace and joy and abundant life. Now take the steps I've outlined and press on forward into your beautiful des- tiny!

— Dr. Arlys McDonald

"I will give thanks to God because I have been so amazingly and miraculously made. Your works are miraculous, and my soul is fully aware of this." – Psalms 139:14

appendix C

FORGIVENESS

What Forgiveness Is:

- Forgiveness is a decision I make to obey God and to walk in His ways.
- Forgiveness is not allowing someone else's actions or attitudes to control or dictate my actions or attitudes.
- A difficult decision. My emotions scream, "No! I can't forgive!" But what I am actually saying is, "I won't forgive."
- Forgiveness is an act of my will. If I do not make this decision, I will have to live with the crippling consequences of my un-forgiveness.
- Forgiveness is getting my own heart right with God.
- Forgiveness is a lifelong lifestyle, not a one-time act. It must be intentional and continuously maintained.
- Realizing a wrong reaction to an offense is just as sinful as the sin against us.
- Forgiveness realizes that my own forgiveness hinges on my willingness to forgive others as soon as possible.
- Forgiveness is a miracle of God working in me.
- Forgiveness is Godliness. It belongs to the ethics of Heaven.
- Forgiveness is a willingness to rebuild a relationship with the one who offended me (in most cases.)
- Forgiveness is to be granted whether or not there is repentance on the part of the one who has offended me.

What Forgiveness Is Not:

- It is not a feeling. It is a decision of my will. (No one feels like forgiving the person or persons that hurt us.)

- Forgiveness is not pretending you were not hurt.
- Forgiveness is not justifying the offender. It is not okay with God for them to hurt you. (Colossians 3:25)
- Forgiveness does not mean you must immediately trust the offender again (i.e. rape, theft.) Forgiveness and trust are two separate issues. We must forgive and then we can work towards trust.
- Forgiveness is not taking vengeance. God will hold each of us accountable. You are responsible for yourself only.
- Forgiveness is NOT easy. It is costly. It cost God everything and it may cost you.

STEPS TO FORGIVENESS

1. Father God, I choose, as an act of my will, to forgive _____ I forgive_____ for_____ (list offenses specifically).
2. Father, I ask that You forgive_____ for these things as well, and that You not hold these charges against him/her on my account. As I release _____, I ask You to release him/her as well.
3. Father, I ask that You forgive me for holding un-forgiveness, bitterness, resentment, etc. in my heart toward _____ I receive Your forgiveness now and Your cleansing of my heart from all unrighteousness.
4. Father, I also choose not to hold any un-forgiveness toward You for allowing these hurts to happen to me. So, I forgive You because I need to and not because You need it.
5. Father God, if there are any more stored-up negative feelings in me toward_____, I ask that you cleanse them from me. I will be open to replace these negative emotions with the fruit of Your Spirit (love, joy, peace, patience, kindness, goodness, faithfulness, gentleness, and self-control).
6. Heavenly Father, I ask that You heal now the wounded places in my soul. Heal my memory of those offenses so that I can look back on them realistically, knowing that they were hurtful, but also knowing that You, Lord, have healed the hurt. Use those experiences for the healing of others with whom I come in contact.
7. Now Father, I ask that you bless_____ with your abundant mercy. Prosper them in every way: mind, body, soul, and spirit.

(Continue to ask God to bless and prosper this person until all negative feelings toward them are healed. Each time you begin to feel anything toward them, use this as a cue to bless and intercede for them.)

Scriptures on Forgiveness: Mark 11:25, 26; Matt. 6:12; Matt. 6:14-15; Eph.4:32; John 20:23

FORGIVENESS WHAT IT IS, WHAT IT ISN'T

Forgiveness **IS NOT** forgetting
Forgiveness **IS NOT** pretending
Forgiveness **IS NOT** a feeling
Forgiveness **IS NOT** bringing up the past
Forgiveness **IS NOT** demanding change before we forgive
Forgiveness **IS** rare, because it is hard
Forgiveness **IS** costly and substitutional

Bringing up the past is destructive, because . . .
- There is nothing you can do to change it.
- It takes away from giving your energy to the present and future.
- It makes you responsible at this point for jeopardizing the marriage or other relationship.
- Even if you were severely offended, by dwelling on the offense you place a continuing burden on your relationship.
- It denies the other party the opportunity to change for the better. This behavior also denies the presence and power of the person of Jesus Christ in a life.
- It does little to elevate you in the eyes of others. An indication of maturity is the desire and willingness to break loose of the past and move forward.

"Be gentle and ready to forgive; never hold grudges. Remember, the Lord forgave you, so you must forgive others." Colossians 3:13

"Your heavenly Father will forgive you if you forgive those who sin against you,

but if you refuse to forgive them, He will not forgive you." Matthew 6:14- 15

"Most of all, continue to show deep love for each other, for love makes up for many of your faults." Peter 4:8

"And we are called to forgive as God has forgiven us. Be as ready to forgive as God for Christ's sake has forgiven you." Ephesians 4:32

"Never pay back evil for evil. Do things in such a way that everyone can see that you are honest clear through." Romans 12:17

FORGIVENESS
THE WRONG WAY, THE RIGHT WAY

THE WRONG WAY
1. I'm sorry IF I was wrong.
2. I'm sorry I did that, I really didn't mean to hurt you.
3. I'm sorry I said what I said, but you were wrong too.
4. I'm sorry. Next time I'll be more careful.

THE RIGHT WAY
I was wrong in what I said or did. Will you please forgive me?

As read on the America Family Living Radio Program, "A Time to Forgive" with Jene and Evie Wilson www.AmericanFamilyLiving.com

appendix D

STEPS TO PEACE WITH GOD

1. God's Plan – Peace and Life
God loves you and wants you to experience His peace and life.

The BIBLE says: *"For God so loved the world that He gave His only begotten Son, that whoever believes in Him should not perish but have everlasting life"* (John 3:16).

2. Our Problem – Separation
Being at peace with God is not automatic, because by Nature you are separated from God.

The BIBLE says: "For all have sinned and fall short of the glory of God" (Romans 3:23).

3. God's Remedy – The Cross
God's love bridges the gap of separation between God and you. When Jesus Christ died on the cross and rose from the grave, He paid the penalty for your sins.

The BIBLE says: *"He personally carried the*

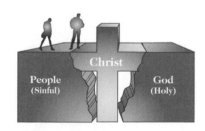

*load of our sins in his own body when he died
on the cross"* (1 Peter 2:24, TLB).

4. Our Response – Receive Christ
You cross the bridge into God's family when you Receive Christ by personal invitation.

The BIBLE says: *"But as many as received Him, to them He gave the right to become children of God, even to those Who believe in His name" (John 1:12).*

*To receive Christ, you need to do four things:
1. ADMIT your spiritual need. "I am a sinner."
2. REPENT and be willing to turn from your sin.
3. BELIEVE that Jesus Christ died for you on the cross.
4. RECEIVE, through prayer, Jesus Christ into your heart and life.

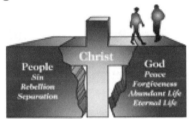

CHRIST says, *"Behold, I stand at the door and knock. If anyone hears My voice and opens the door, I will come in"* (Revelation 3:20).

The BIBLE says, *"Whoever calls upon the name of the Lord will be saved"* (Romans 10:13).

What to Pray:
Dear Lord Jesus, I know that I am a sinner and need Your forgiveness. I believe that You died for my sins. I want to turn from my sins. I now invite You to come into my heart and life. I want to trust and follow You as Lord and Savior. In Jesus' name, Amen.

HOPE + HEALING

·············· *to victims of trauma **everywhere!*** ··············

LION & THE LAMB LIFEPACKS

In 2016, ATP began delivering Lion And The Lamb comfort toys to children in the Middle East and has now delivered over 22,000 toys. These toys bring comfort and healing to children that have experienced severe trauma.

IMMEDIATE TRAUMA NEEDS

ATP leverages its global following to raise emergency support funds for those in need. ATP recently supported seven families in need of shelter in Northern Iraq and launched an online campaign to sponsor surgery for a 16 year-old Iraqi girl on her birthday.

STATESIDE OUTREACH

Victor is a renowned speaker and master of martial arts. He connects to youth and adults through his powerful testimony, martial arts skills and important messages from his work overseas. Victor continues to reach broken youth and families across North America.

VICTORMARX
ALL THINGS POSSIBLE MINISTRIES

Post Office Box 63176
Colorado Springs, CO 80962

DONATE AT
VictorMarx.com
ReachChildren.com